C000147378

WALKING IN KENT
VOL I

St Edith's Well, a colourful corner of Kemsing. (Walk 3)

WALKING IN KENT
VOL I

by

KEV REYNOLDS

CICERONE PRESS
MILNTHORPE, CUMBRIA

© Kev Reynolds
ISBN 1 85284 192 3
First published 1988 (ISBN 1 85284 004 8)
Second edition 1995
A catalogue record for this book is available from the British Library.

*In memory of Margaret Grummant,
a good friend who loved the countryside - everywhere.
And in thanks to my wife who shared every walk
and made the sun shine.*

Cicerone Press guidebooks by the same author:
    Walking in Kent - Vol II
    The Wealdway & The Vanguard Way
    The South Downs Way & The Downs Link
    The Cotswold Way
    Walks & Climbs in the Pyrenees
    Walks in the Engadine - Switzerland
    The Jura (with R B Evans)
    The Valais - Switzerland
    The Bernese Alps
    Central Switzerland
    Ticino - Switzerland
    Alpine Pass Route
    Chamonix to Zermatt - the Walker's Haute Route
    Annapurna - a Trekker's Guide
    Everest - a Trekker's Guide

Front Cover: The best way to reach Lamberhurst church from the village
    is by a series of cross-country footpaths. (Walk 33)

CONTENTS

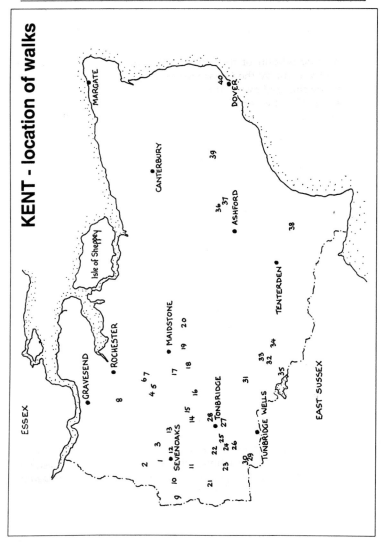

KENT - location of walks

PREFACE TO THE SECOND EDITION

As the first edition of this guidebook went to press, Southern England was hit by the Great Storm of 16 October 1987, and the landscape changed overnight.

Much of Kent was badly affected. Many footpaths described in the book became impassable, blocked as they were by fallen trees. Some of the walks were scrapped before publication. Others were necessarily re-routed in places. Visiting areas one had known and loved for decades was often a heart-breaking experience; in places views were bewilderingly different to those we remembered.

But time is a great healer, of landscapes as of men, and the countryside has reshaped itself with the seasonal restlessness of nature. Thanks to the hard work of farmers, landowners, council workmen and teams of volunteers, footpaths were soon reopened and the scenic splendours of Kent restored - not necessarily as they were, but certainly no less lovely than before.

It's good, then, to have an opportunity to rewalk these routes and describe them afresh, to discover 'new' scenes and delight once more to the pleasures of this county of ours. It is, of course, under constant threat - not only from the excesses of the weather, but from commercial and industrial development, from new homes, out-of-town shopping centres, from a seemingly unchecked road-building programme, from the Channel Tunnel Rail Link, and from the 'stone-in-a-pond' effects of the Chunnel itself. Perhaps if more of us realised just how good, but vulnerable, this countryside is, enough voices would be raised to help save some of it for future generations.

Walking the footpaths of Kent will reveal the best of the county and underline how important it is to save it. In a book published recently to illustrate the changing face of the county, the author and his photographers showed the negative side. It was a powerful commentary on the destruction of the Garden of England, in which the author asked if it were possible to walk anywhere in Kent away from the sound of traffic. This book is an answer to that question! It also provides a positive view. By knowing what glories there are at risk, let's make sure the risks diminish and the glories increase.

*   *   *

The first edition of *Walking in Kent* met with an encouraging response and a lively postbag. I am grateful to all who wrote to say how much they'd enjoyed exploring our countryside, who asked for another volume (published 1994), who pointed out changes that had occurred on a number of walks and made suggestions for this second edition. Having walked all the routes again with my wife, I've been able to incorporate many of these suggestions. Some have been changed slightly, and two new routes have been included to help ease the geographical balance. I hope they will bring you as much pleasure as they gave me, not only when out walking, but rewalking them by finger tip across the keyboard of my word-processor.

Kev Reynolds

ADVICE TO READERS

Readers are advised that whilst every effort is taken by the author to ensure the accuracy of this guidebook, changes can occur which may affect the contents. A book of this nature with detailed descriptions and detailed maps is more prone to change than a more general guide. New fences and stiles appear, waymarking alters, there may be new buildings or eradication of old buildings. It is advisable to check locally on transport, accommodation, shops etc. but even rights of way can be altered, paths can be eradicated by landslip, forest clearances or changes of ownership. The publisher would welcome notes of any such changes.

Apple blossom will brighten any walk in spring

INTRODUCTION

My window looks out at what once was an orchard. Several apple trees still stand there, and as I write they are in full blossom. Bullfinches dart to and fro among them, threatening to limit this summer's fruit. A nuthatch scrambles head-down in search of insects on the trunk of one of the trees while a magpie bounces across the lawn.

Beyond the apple trees there's a screen of sycamore, chestnut, oak, beech and pine. Bluebells collect at their ankles, and through the lush new foliage there comes the faint hint of distance. Out there beyond the trees, beyond the bluebells and juicy shoots of next month's cow parsley, lies the Weald of Kent. Or part of it.

Behind the village rise the greensand hills. They form one of the highest parts of Kent, and one of the loveliest of all the county's natural features. I can be on that ridge of hills within a few short minutes, wandering footpaths that trace a line of splendour through woods and into hidden vales and over breezy hilltops that have known all the years of man's involvement in these isles. London is but twenty miles or so away - not the suburbs, but the very heart of it. Yet from this ridge one would never know it, for the eye is drawn into a deep and vast sweep of greenery without a town in sight, with no motorway or tower block or sprawl of modern shopping centre. A vast sweep of greenery it is, of woodland and meadow and fields put to corn. There are one or two vineyards and orchards and hop gardens. But they are lost among the broader mass of trees. Down there, hidden in the vast acreage of the Weald, there are tiny villages as picturesque as any you'll find in Britain. There are magnificent stately homes and castles bearing in their sturdy walls part of the nation's history. And there are country cottages with honeysuckle over their doors and streams chuckling through their gardens. Footpaths lead to them and past them as they have for hundreds of years, serving as byways for all our ancestors.

In ancient parklands deer nibble at the grass where once princes and poets strolled - troubadors of another time. In wood-lined meadows rabbits wash their faces in the dew of early morning. There are badger setts making a honeycomb of the hillside. Foxes roam the fields on trackways worn over several generations, squirrels race overhead on a trellis of branches. There are jays screeching, pheasants exploding from the cover of a hedgerow. Soon there'll be butterflies drifting in a summer breeze, toads belching by green ponds on the edge of a secluded farmyard. And wild flowers everywhere.

*   *   *

Almost every day for two decades and more I've found an excuse to wander the footpaths of Kent. Not just those on my doorstep, but others a little farther afield, too; walking to meetings held a dozen miles or so away; walking to evensong at a neighbouring parish church; walking for the simple pleasure of the exercise. Often I've walked alone, at my own pace, not caring where the pathways led so long as they gave a breath of fresh air, a taste of nature's kingdom, a glimpse of heaven. Seldom have I been disappointed. Even in a full-blown gale or a steady downpour it has transpired that once outside, the elements were much more acceptable than when viewed from the warmth of a sitting room. In fine weather or foul nature has gifts on offer.

Sometimes I've had company. Then it's been good to share these landscapes, these intimate scenes and special places, with others. Sometimes I've led groups eager to discover the secrets of our countryside. Groups of children on nature rambles, boggle-eyed with wonder at the owl-pellets found beneath an oak tree, at the flavour of different leaves, at the contrasting scents to be discovered at the mouths of badger setts and fox's earths. There were also groups of adults loath, perhaps, to explore on their own, but who needed the company of someone familiar with the area to direct them.

Once there was a group of senior citizens on an evening ramble in spring. I took them on a short stroll across a rolling meadowland and up onto one of our local hills. We wandered through an archway of beeches with a million bluebells at our feet, and sat with a view to the west and watched the sun go down. In twilight we then crossed the crown of the hill where pheasants were roosting on the branches of a clump of pine trees, their tails hanging down to make a frieze of feathers. All views to east and south were by then dusted with shadow, and we returned downhill to the village in full darkness, in single file holding hands along a rough, unseen track that could only be felt under foot. There was a fragrance in the air that told of plants moist with night dew. Far off came the bleating of sheep.

*   *   *

This guidebook has been written to encourage others to step out along the footpaths of this lovely county in the hope that they, too, may respond to the riches it holds. Forty walks are not many from the hundreds of possibilities that exist, but they serve as a pointer, a nudge in the right direction. The majority are found in western Kent, along the North Downs and the Greensand Ridge, in the valleys of the Eden and the Medway, and in the Weald. I make no apology for this. This is country I know best of all; it's on my doorstep and on the doorstep of countless thousands of other countryside walkers too. Consequently, most of the paths described are reasonably well-used and should be easy to follow. With the exception of only two, all walks are circular. Most are fairly short in favour of those who prefer a half-day outing to a full day's expedition.

But a number are linked, so it is possible in these cases to join two half-day walks together, should you feel the need for additional exercise.

Walking in the countryside is most rewarding when conducted at a leisurely pace. There will always be something of interest to look at, or listen to, or sniff at. There will often be a surprise view to linger over; a moment to reflect on the good fortune that brings us out into fine country; an opportunity to get life into perspective. So half a dozen miles of countryside wandering may lead to as many hours of activity. Who cares? Walk with an eye on the world about you, not on the clock.

This is a book for all who suddenly feel that an hour or so of fresh air and fine scenery would ease a burden, 'clear the cobwebs' and help face life head-on once more. It's also for the keen weekend rambler, hoping that within these pages there will be a discovery or two to be made; for others too, who would not consider themselves to be walkers at all, but who may be tempted one day to leave the car behind and take a peep over the hill, or round the woodland, or along the river bank.

Wandering the gentle footpaths of Kent has brought me as much pleasure as scrambling on some of Europe's more dramatic mountains, or trekking in Africa or the high Himalaya. Through them I have discovered that the world about us has a diversity that rewards those who willingly discard the blinkers of specialisation. For me, an hour in the countryside gives an opportunity to glimpse a vision of glory.

May you, through the pages of this guide, be led to a discovery of some of that glory too.

KENT - A WALKER'S COUNTY

Kent is a large and complex county, a great county for the lover of fine scenery. Particularly is it rewarding for the walker, for whilst there may be no mountains to provide the degree of high drama for which the Lake District and Snowdonia are noted, nor moorlands of windswept mystery such as those of Yorkshire or the south-west, Kent's own subtle brand of gentleness seems to embody the very essence of the British countryside. Here, in its wooded hills and valleys, in the cultivated acres of the Weald, along the soft chalk downlands and lofty greensand, and the low-lying levels of Romney Marsh, can be found a mirror to the very uniqueness of England: its diversity.

Kent offers a series of landscapes that are not only colourful, varied and rich in history but, of importance to the walker, they are accessible. Many hundreds of miles of footpath await exploration, the majority of which are clearly defined and well marked with finger-posts or direction stones, with stiles and swing gates and footbridges over streams. Through them there's no better way of understanding the countryside than by slowly moving towards its heart. There's no finer way of learning about a county than by deserting its roads and towns and taking to its footpaths. They lead where no motorised traveller can go, into a world peopled by animals, insects and birds along routes that form the very arteries of that countryside, and which grant an opportunity to feel the pulse of that land. They will take us into scenes straight out of the history books and give us a glimpse of the future too. In Kent's countryside there are many lessons for us all to learn.

The county may be divided conveniently into geographical regions dominated by its main features. First the North Downs, that long ridge of chalk that spreads right across the county from its north-western border with Surrey to the south-eastern majesty of the White Cliffs of Dover. Along this almost continuous escarpment there are just four breaks in Kent: north of Sevenoaks where the Darent flows through, near Maidstone to make way for the Medway, at Wye where the Great Stour has forced a passage en route to Canterbury, and east of Canterbury by the Little Stour.

Running almost parallel with the downs is the Greensand Ridge. The hills that fashion this ridge form a sort of inner lining to the North Downs and a wall confining the Weald. They are not the downs, nor of the downs, but as with the downs their northern slopes are gentle, while the southern edge plunges steeply from a wooded escarpment. In places this scarp slope forms concave sides, and in certain areas there have been dramatic landslips: at Crockham Hill and Toys Hill, for example.

Then there is the Weald itself, a vast clay basin that contains the Garden of England and which once formed such an obstacle to the Romans. They called it *Anderida*. Then it was a great forest; now

15

there are hop gardens and vineyards, orchards and wheatfields and rolling meadows flecked with a cumulus of grazing sheep. The Low Weald, heavy under foot in wet weather, almost completely surrounds the belt of hills of the High Weald, an attractive region of husbandry with spectacular views from villages such as Brenchley, Goudhurst and Lamberhurst.

At the southern end of the county lies that strange, level, low-lying region of Romney Marsh - land that once was sea. There, where water-courses run dye-straight, all seems bent to the horizon - the trees and hedgerows and even the churches themselves, of which the marsh has a notable collection, appear to huddle in resistance to winds that blow unchecked by high ground from the sea.

And there's coastal Kent, too. Whilst we may note in the marsh country Kent's gain from the sea, and remark on the ever-changing land, it is along the coastline that we see the most dramatic alterations that have taken place over many centuries. Nothing illustrates this better than the route of the Saxon Shore Way, for in many places this long-distance footpath wanders along green slopes of meadowland where once the waves pounded against sea cliffs; walking today where not so long ago ships sailed; flowers and trees growing where the Danes brought their longships on raiding parties and Men of Kent lived in fear of invasion from a sea that now has tractors ploughing waves of rich soil. Conversely there are sea lanes today where our Saxon forefathers built their defences, and where before them the legions of Rome tramped in orderly file, creating links between centres of commerce and administration.

One may gain a hint of these things from geography or history books and maps and photographs. The motorist may drive along roadways that trace some of the glories of Kent and glimpse a taste of its heartland. But only the walker can truly understand what diverse and spectacular forms the countryside adopts. Wander through the remaining beechwoods that crown the Greensand Ridge and come suddenly to their southern tip. There you will be confronted by an enormous panorama, as lovely as any you'd wish to find in England, with the Weald far below, a world of green leading off to smokey blue distance. There are many such places in this guide where moments of surprise and wonder will take your breath.

Or across the bald downs above Kemsing or Wye, cropped downland grass starred with flowers and alive with butterflies, with pathways that have borne the feet of prehistoric ramblers, and imagine the world as it was then. Our footpaths take us to their burial grounds where we wrestle with imagination as we attempt to understand how they manhandled multi-ton blocks of stone one on top of another four thousand years ago.

In the Weald we may be led to a discovery of hidden furnace ponds where once Britain's iron industry was in full smelt, but today only birds break the silence of a leaf-wrapped sanctuary. In many places we find more than a hint of the iron trade that so changed the face of the Weald. There are deep, sunken lanes that were made by heavily laden waggons drawn by oxen. Carting stone and iron through the clay hills they left their mark printed indelibly on the land. In streams we see the rust-red shine that indicates the presence of ironstone, and find magnificent country houses nearby that were built by the iron-masters of yesteryear.

Kent boasts some 24,000 historic buildings. They're not all castles and cathedrals, nor stately homes, of course, although the county has its fair share of these. More often than not they're old-world cottages, tile-hung or timber-framed. Some of them are wonderful hall houses, planted in the generous soil that helped their builders prosper. Not all are accessible to the public. By far the majority are hidden away from prying eyes and well aimed cameras. But the wanderer of footpaths has a privileged view, for so often a walk will lead beside an historic building, through grounds that would otherwise be kept firmly closed with a private sign to deter the inquisitive. The footpath is our passport to roam, and we gain another insight into this county's secrets that no-one who travels only by car will ever know.

There are outcrops of sandstone hidden in this countryside that may also be found only by taking to the footpaths. There are unmarked caves too, and springs of clear water used by Iron Age man. There are ancient hillforts and Roman villas along some of our walks, and magical places that nature has created out of sight of roadway or village, that only the observant walker will find. Such discoveries await the footpath wanderer in Kent.

In springtime there's the heady fragrance of bluebell, wild garlic and cow parsley. Buds quiver around us, and we wander through woodlands showered by discarded husks as new leaves open. There will be birdsong, and a special vibrancy as the countryside pulls itself out of winter sloth.

The warm air of summer draws moisture from field and woodland; could we but sit on a hill and watch that rainfall in reverse! Yet in the woods the very air seems green, so that the footpaths we tread may almost be under the sea. In these woods then there is welcome shade, and it's always worth taking a few moments to observe the industrious hustling of insects - on the path and on the trunks of trees.

Autumn of course replaces green with yellow and gold. Late in the day we stroll out of the hills and down into pockets of cool air and mist among pheasants, heavy-bellied and ignorant as to their winter fate. And in winter these same paths take us into a new-found openness as we discover broad vistas where in summer the leaf-bound trees limited our field of vision.

Every season has its own special gifts. Every corner of Kent its own special flavour.

TRANSPORT AND ACCOMMODATION

The decline in public transport in rural areas since the late 'sixties is to be regretted.

However, there are still bus services in Kent that stray to surprisingly remote villages, although these services may be limited to just one or two days a week. It would not be wise to quote specific details here as changes are made with alarming frequency, but you are advised to check with individual operators for up-to-date details.

The railway network which cuts across the county may be of considerable use to walkers without their own transport. In addition to mainline routes linking London with the coast, there are minor lines, such as that which runs from Redhill through the Eden Valley via Edenbridge, Penshurst and Leigh to Tonbridge, and another from East Croydon through Edenbridge Town, Hever, Cowden and Ashurst. There are convenient routes through Paddock Wood to Maidstone, and another which cuts across the northern part of the county to the Medway Towns. But how any of these will be affected by privatisation, one may only speculate.

It is worth noting that a number of rural stations are actually situated some miles from the village named on their boards, and if used you may find that your walking mileage is markedly increased as a consequence.

A word of warning to motorists may not be out of place concerning car parking in remote areas. Whilst most of these walks begin in a village or small town where there will be adequate parking facilities, some outings necessitate leaving vehicles in an isolated lay-by or woodland car park without supervision. Kent is no more nor less susceptible to thefts from cars than other counties, but it is always worth making doubly sure that vehicles are left as secure as possible. Never leave valuables in the car, nor any obvious sign that it's being left for some time.

When parking in a village where there is no public car park, please be considerate to locals and make sure you do not obstruct access to houses, farms or fields. Similarly, if you should choose to park near a church, do take note of the likelihood of the church being used for a service whilst you're away, and park accordingly. Church users must take priority where there is limited space; after all, it is often they who pay for the creation and upkeep of the parking area. Give consideration to others, and let discretion be your guide.

As for accommodation suitable for walkers, Kent at present has just three youth hostels: at Canterbury, Dover and Kemsing. Membership of YHA (England and Wales) can be arranged by writing to the National Office whose address is given in the Appendix. Up-to-date details of facilities, prices and opening times are given in the YHA Guide which comes free with membership.

Bed and breakfast accommodation is available across the county. The Ramblers' Association *Yearbook* lists recommended addresses, but more specifically Kent County Council publishes a brochure containing hundreds of addresses of hotels, motels, guest houses, b&b, self-catering and farm accommodation, as well as camping and caravan sites; a very useful publication.

Walkers beware! This bull is happily disinterested - for the moment

NOTES FOR WALKERS

No specialised equipment is necessary for wandering Kent's footpaths, but if you plan to go walking on a frequent basis it would be worth buying a decent pair of lightweight boots. In any case footwear should be comfortable, whether you wear boots, shoes, trainers or wellingtons. Some of the walks included in this book were surveyed in dry conditions when trainers would have been adequate. On some walks wellington boots were a definite advantage as I sloshed along green lanes that were anything but. Conditions underfoot change quickly, and it is probably only those who live in the countryside and are familiar with their locality who will know what is suitable footwear for their paths at any given time. My suggestion would be to wear wellington boots (with a comfortable fit) in winter, and trainers or walking boots for the rest of the year.

Shorts may be fine on some walks, but in summer brambles or nettles often invade across the pathway, and in such instances long trousers are preferred. Few will risk walking far in our unsettled climate without having some form of waterproof jacket or cagoule with them. A pair of lightweight overtrousers can be particularly handy for crossing fields of tall crops after rain, or in the early morning following a heavy dew.

If you're unused to walking far, take along a pack of plasters in case of blisters, and for the odd scratch or two. An Ordnance Survey map will be most helpful - as long as you know how to interpret it - not only as an aid should you become lost, but to bring added life to the countryside through which you travel. Details of specific sheets required for each walk are provided.

On a long day-walk I always carry a few sandwiches and an apple for lunch, as I'd much rather picnic beneath a tree with a view than stop at a pub. However, I've noted the presence of pubs where they occur for the benefit of those with a preference for liquid refreshment. Many pubs offer snacks or more substantial meals, of course, but it should be pointed out that not all landlords welcome ramblers - and having seen how much clay can be picked up on walking boots after a mile of Wealden wandering, I can sympathise with some of the excuses put foward to deter them. Be prepared to cover your boots with polythene bags, or remove them completely before entering a pub or café.

Mention of any pub or café in this guide must not be taken as a personal endorsement of the services on offer.

One naturally assumes that anyone setting out on a walk through the countryside will be a country lover to some degree. The more surprising it is, then, to find pieces of litter where only walkers can go. We all have a responsibility towards the land in which we live and walk, so should do our bit towards reducing the impact of litter. Not only by making sure we leave none ourselves, but by taking home with us a little of that left by others. That way we each can make a positive response, no matter how small the immediate overall effect might appear. Perhaps then some farmers may feel guilty over discarded fertiliser bags left in hedgerow and ditch, and the rusting pieces of machinery being steadily strangled by the briar!

Practically every walk in this guide involves wandering through agricultural land of some sort, so please be careful to avoid damaging crops. Paths may not always be abundantly clear on the ground, but directions have been given to enable you to locate the correct route.

Clear advice in a sheep-raising county

If your path goes through a field of growing crops, walk in single file to minimise the effect. And remember, hay is a crop too, not just 'long grass'. Treat such fields as you would those of ripening wheat.

Sheep graze many Kentish meadowlands. Take care not to panic them, especially when they are in lamb. Keep dogs under close control, and on a lead where there is livestock.

Some of our walks traverse golf courses, and when on such an outing it's worth keeping extra vigilant, especially when crossing a fairway.

USING THE GUIDE

Sketch maps that accompany each route description provide a basic outline, but are no substitute for an Ordnance Survey map. A note is given with regard to the O.S. sheets which cover each individual walk. In the first edition only the 1:50,000 scale (1^1/$_4$" = 1 mile) Landranger maps were mentioned, but for this book I also provide a note of the Pathfinder series which, at a scale of 1:25,000, give much more detail. A grid reference (GR) is also quoted in places to help locate your exact position with some ease.

Certain words used in the descriptions may not be familiar to townsfolk, so the following brief glossary is offered in explanation.

coppice   an area of woodland trees, usually consisting of hazel or sweet chestnut, harvested in a cycle of anything from seven to twenty years. When harvested, trees are cut back to a stump from which new growth rises. Coppiced timber is used for a variety of purposes, including fencing. In the past Kent's coppice woodlands produced timber for hop poles and hurdles.

headland   the edge of a field which the farmer has left rough and unploughed. It not only enables walkers to ease round a field without damaging crops, but also provides a habitat for numerous small mammals and is often rich in wild flowers.

pollard   similar to coppicing, but here trees are cut about six feet above the ground. Very little pollarding is done in Britain today, other than for ornamental purposes, but several of Kent's oldest woodlands contain fine examples.

shaw   a strip of woodland, usually separating two fields.

Throughout this guide I have sought to give additional information on interesting places or features seen along the way. In the text these are marked with a cross-reference number, information

23

being outlined at the end of the walk description corresponding with this text number. Several are open to the public, either through the auspices of the National Trust or English Heritage. Opening times are not given as they can vary from year to year. Up-to-date details can be obtained from a number of annual publications as well from the organisations responsible.

By far the majority of paths described are Public Rights of Way. In one or two instances footpaths are used by courtesy of the landowner. From time to time diversion orders are made, so routes may vary slightly from those shown on the O.S. map. It should also be pointed out that some stiles used during route surveys were found to be in a decrepit condition. They may be replaced by other stiles, or even by a gate by the time you walk them. Apart from such minor changes, it may well be that certain landmarks such as isolated trees will be felled by storm or a farmer's axe. Other landmarks, such as farm reservoirs, may appear where none is seen today. Agricultural dictates from the E.C. may lead to even more farmland being turned into golf courses, or become haggard through set-aside. We may even (heaven forbid) be battered by another hurricane! Should you find that a section of a walk has seriously changed for one reason or another, I'd very much appreciate a note giving specific details, and I'll check it out for any subsequent edition. Correspondence may be forwarded to me c/o the publisher.

*   *   *

Finally, please observe the Country Code:

1: Enjoy the countryside and respect its life and work.
2: Guard against all risk of fire.
3: Fasten all gates.
4: Keep dogs under close control.
5: Keep to public paths across farmland.
6: Use gates and stiles to cross fences, hedges and walls.
7: Leave livestock, crops and machinery alone.
8: Take your litter home.
9: Help to keep all water clean.
10: Protect wildlife, plants and trees.
11: Take special care on country roads.
12: Make no unnecessary noise.

It was Octavia Hill, that indomitable champion of the countryside and co-founder of the National Trust (who spent some of her happiest days along the Greensand Ridge), whose words at the turn of the century sum up the spirit of the Country Code:

> "Let the grass growing for hay be respected,
> let the primrose roots be left in their loveliness
> in the hedges, the birds unmolested and the gates shut.
> If those who frequented country places
> would consider those who live there,
> they would better deserve, and more often retain,
> the rights and privileges they enjoy."

Shoreham, on the River Darent. (Walks 1 & 2)

The Darent and The Downs

The North Downs enter Kent from Surrey just outside Westerham and immediately reach the county's highest point at Betsom's Hill, around 800 feet above sea level. The chalk ridge then arcs towards the north-east, a tremendous scarp giving sudden plunging views to the south, but easing in the north and sloping gently into London's land-hungry suburbs. The downs have somehow managed to limit the southward growth of the capital, and at the same time retained a real taste of countryside on the very fringe of suburbia.

To the south of Westerham the little River Darent rises among the greensand hills. It then sifts through a sheltered valley known as Squerryes Park, enters Westerham among well tended gardens, and then swings to the east. On its journey towards Sevenoaks, linking the villages of the Holmesdale Valley, the Darent makes little impact, except on infrequent occasions when it bursts its banks and causes distress to a few unfortunate householders. But by the time it reaches Otford this insignificant stream has changed direction again, veering north now on its way towards the Thames. Over who-knows-how-many thousands of years it has carved a great breach in the otherwise imposing wall of the downs.

Between Otford and Farningham downstream, the Darent Valley is a charming swathe of greenery. A few orchards and hop gardens adorn the valley bed, with steep slopes of downland on either side. There are storm-thinned woodlands along the crown of the hills which happily screen the excesses of the motorway builder and save this delightful area for another day.

The Romans were active throughout the valley, and at Lullingstone, between Shoreham and Eynsford, the remains of a splendid Roman villa containing an early Christian chapel are on display to the public, while in Eynsford village the ruins of a former Norman castle, built on the banks of the Darent, have pieces of Roman tile in their walls.

East of the Darent's valley the North Downs wallow in a great swell of chalk field and meadow once more. On their edges some lovely walks offer extensive views over the agricultural land below. Trosley Country Park was established by Kent County Council along the scarp edge here as a large recreational area above the village of Trottiscliffe. With its large space for car parking, its information centre, woodland and waymarked trails, the Park makes an obvious base for a day's excursion.

To the north and east of Trosley, in the peaceful 'heartland' of the downs, there are walks to be had into seemingly lost valleys and through colourful woods that have known a chequered history. At Luddesdown there stands a house that has been continuously lived in since the days of the Conqueror, when William's Bishop Odo took up residence. And a few fields away, at the end of a narrow no-through-road, there stands a sorry little barn-like church whose parish disappeared with the Black Death in 1349.

Through this countryside pass the routes of several long-distance paths: the Wealdway, London Countryway, North Downs Way and the Pilgrims Way. With so much industry and housing conurbation nearby, the apparent seclusion of this corner of the county, as explored by the footpath walker, will come as a surprise - and a welcome one at that.

*   *   *

WALK 1: OTFORD - SHOREHAM - OTFORD

Distance:	5½ miles
Maps:	O.S. Pathfinder 1208 'Sevenoaks & Westerham' and 1192 'Orpington' 1:25,000
	O.S. Landranger 188 'Maidstone & The Weald of Kent' 1:50,000
Start:	Otford High Street (GR: 525594)
Access:	A225 north of Sevenoaks for about 2 miles. Nearest railway station: Otford
Parking:	By the village hall opposite The Bull Inn
Refreshments:	Pubs in Otford and Shoreham

There are two distinct phases to this walk. The first follows the Darent Valley Path alongside the stream, initially on its right bank with willows

28

draping themselves over the water in true romantic fashion, veers away a little and takes a route over fields and alongside a hedgerow beside the fairways of a golf course, then into Shoreham to rejoin the stream once more. The second phase tackles the downs rising to the west of the valley. Having gained their upper slopes, the footpath traverses back towards the south, enjoying long views ahead, across the Darent Gap, and down to orchards below, before descending to the valley for a final across-the-fields section back to Otford. This makes a very pleasant outing, incorporating as it does the two main features of this corner of the county: the Darent and the downs.

*   *   *

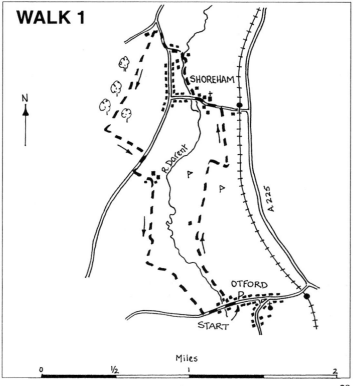

WALK 1

N

SHOREHAM

R. Darent

A 225

OTFORD

START

Miles

0   ½   1   2

Leave the car park opposite The Bull Inn, turn right and walk along Otford High Street (1) until you come to the Darent stream. A Darent Valley Path (2) marker post stands at the entrance to a driveway on the right and signifies the proper start to our walk. Wander along the driveway towards some houses under which the Darent flows - an attractive sight. When it forks take the right-hand option beside a converted oast house. A footpath continues from it and leads into a field. Wander ahead beside the stream which is shallow and clear as it flows beneath old willows in indolent fashion.

At the far side of this first field cross a stile and desert the Darent to walk straight ahead over the next open field. Reach and cross a track serving as the drive to a house on the left, and maintain direction with views along the valley. In the west the gently sloping wall of the North Downs rises above orchards and oasts. Some way ahead a large chalk cross can be seen carved in the downland slope. This is Shoreham's war memorial, and on the return journey our walk will pass immediately above it.

The path continues in the same direction keeping a fairly straight line alongside a hedgerow, and is then guided by fences and Darent Valley Path waymarks across a golf course. On reaching a broad trackway turn right for about 250 yards, then bear left at cross-tracks. An enclosed footpath now takes you to a cricket pitch, and on through a swing gate for a further section of enclosed path which leads to a golf course fairway (caution when crossing), and eventually onto a road (GR: 524615). Turn left and walk into Shoreham village (3).

The road twists between the Old George Inn and the entrance to the parish church of St Peter and St Paul where John Wesley preached on several occasions, and passing a number of cottages rejoins the Darent stream. Two branches of the stream unite under an attractive hump-backed bridge, with a stone war memorial beside it. Bear right immediately before the bridge and soon come to the entrance to The Water House, where Samuel Palmer, the landscape artist lived for about seven years. Veer left past the entrance and follow the stream again as it flows among willows at the foot of a row of gardens. The way now crosses the stream on a footbridge, and in a few yards reaches a driveway leading to a white house set on the bank of the stream.

Leave the Darent Valley Path here, and walk up Mill Lane, at the top of which you come to a road junction and some flint cottages. Turn right for about 300 yards, the road winding steadily uphill soon becoming a sunken lane walled by high banks with trees overhanging.

Come to a footpath breaking away left beside a curious small meadow backed by a chalk bank which appears to have once been a quarry. Go up this path, and on reaching the top turn immediately to the left (in effect almost doubling-back on yourself) on a track which swings to the right after a few yards. After a while the track forks by a notice board announcing Meenfield Wood. Continue ahead on what is the left-hand option, enjoying fine views across the Darent Valley to the eastern wall of the downs, and far ahead to the Greensand Ridge blocking all hint of the Weald that lies beyond that.

The way continues to rise easily along the hillside. Through a gap in the hedge there is a view down onto the top of the large war memorial cross carved in the chalk, with a stone tablet bearing the inscription:

'To the creator, in gratitude for all those men of Shoreham who lost their lives in the 1914-1918 war.'

The way continues on a belvedere course, but views become restricted for a while until you reach a field gate with a stile next to it. Cross this and turn left to drop downhill on a path that leads to an enclosed track - once more with lovely views along the valley - bringing you to Filston Lane where you turn right (GR: 515611).

After about 100 yards pass the driveway leading to Filston Oast (4), and in another 70 yards come to the entrance to Filston Farm. Immediately beyond the farm drive turn left on a footpath alongside a hedgerow. Bear right in front of a barn, then left down the end of it, passing other farm buildings to reach a track beyond. This soon curves to the right and when it narrows to a footpath you continue ahead along the left-hand edge of a large field.

On the far side come onto another track and bear left. In a few paces veer slightly to the right away from the track on a path which edges a fenced field. This path is raised above the right-hand fields,

Detail on a door in Otford

and it brings you to a footbridge over a brook. Over this the way swings left then right again to resume along the right-hand edge of another field. A stile gives access to the next field where you follow the left-hand boundary to yet another stile in the hedge ahead. Over this maintain direction to a road (The Pilgrims Way). Bear left and wander along it into Otford village.

Items of interest:

1: Otford. This historic village was settled by the Romans some 2,000 years ago. Various pieces of mosaic and tile have been found here dating from the earlier occupation. But in A.D. 774 a great battle was fought here between Offa, King of Mercia, and the Men of Kent. Again, in 1016, Otford was the scene of bloodshed when the Danes fought a pitched battle on the site of Offa's field. Much later, one of Tudor England's finest mansions was built here to house successive Archbishops of Canterbury on their travels. Becket was in Otford, so was Cranmer, but today the Archbishop's Palace is little more than a ruin set back from a too-busy road near the church.

2: Darent Valley Path. A 15-mile walk leads alongside the Darent stream from Riverhead (or Chipstead) on the outskirts of Sevenoaks, to Dartford on the Thames. It is waymarked throughout, and with four linking circular walks described in a pack entitled: *Countryside Walks in North West Kent.*

3: Shoreham. One of the most attractive villages in the Darent Valley, it has links with John Wesley, William Blake and Samuel Palmer. Wesley preached here, and Blake visited Palmer when he

Trottiscliffe's church slumbers in a hollow below the downs. (Walks 4 & 5)
The Leather Bottle Inn at Cobham appears in novels by Dickens. (Walk 8)

The buildings of Froghole are draped on the slopes of Mariners Hill. (Walk 9)
Ightham Mote, one of Kent's finest old buildings, is now in the care of the
National Trust. (Walks 12 &14)

lived at The Water House. Another of Palmer's friends, Edward Calvert, once wrote that the Darent Valley was "so hidden from the world that the devil has not yet found it". Shoreham was also home to Verney Lovett Cameron, the explorer who was the first man to cross Africa from one side to the other. His father was rector of Shoreham for many years.

4: Filston Hall. Standing down by the Darent to the south of Shoreham, this Tudor mansion house has a moat round it formed by diverting the stream.

WALK 2: LULLINGSTONE PARK - SHOREHAM - LULLINGSTONE PARK

Distance:	6¹/₂ miles
Maps:	O.S. Pathfinder 1192 'Orpington' 1:25,000
	O.S. Landranger 177 'East London Area' 1:50,000
Start:	Lullingstone Park Visitor Centre (GR: 526638)
Access:	Via Castle Road cutting south-west off A225 ¹/₂ mile south of Eynsford railway bridge. The Visitor Centre stands at the sharp bend ¹/₂ mile down Castle Road. Nearest railway station: Eynsford
Parking:	At the Visitor Centre
Refreshments:	Cafeteria at the Visitor Centre; bar & restaurant at Lullingstone Park Golf Course; pubs in Shoreham

Lullingstone Park provides a focus of outdoor recreation on the west flank of the Darent Valley between Shoreham and Eynsford. In addition to the ubiquitous golf course, there are woodland walks and fine views from open meadows, while the Visitor Centre on the bank of the Darent stream serves the public with refreshments, toilet facilities, interpretive leaflets, walking guides and plenty of information about the natural history of the area.

In addition to the pleasures of the North Downs, there are many other interesting features to this walk. First a riverside stroll, views across a man-made lake to the mis-named Lullingstone Castle, then an opportunity to make a short diversion to see the remains of a Roman villa. There are handsome farmhouses and flint-walled cottages, an imposing mansion set in neat lawns, and a rather striking viaduct marching across the valley.

*   *   *

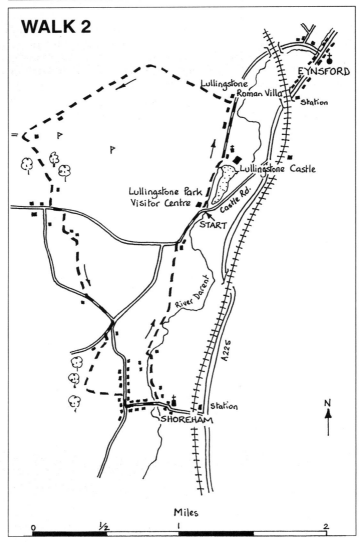

WALK 2

EYNSFORD

Lullingstone
Roman Villa

Station

Lullingstone Castle

Lullingstone Park
Visitor Centre

Castle Rd.

START

River Darent

A225

SHOREHAM

Station

N

Miles

0   ½   1   2

Leave the car park at its entrance, and bear left along the tree-lined path which traces the left bank of the Darent. Beyond the stream can be seen a large lake that extends as far as the red-brick Lullingstone Castle (1). Passing a weir the path leads through a small parking area and onto a lane. Wander ahead for almost ½ mile. Immediately before reaching Lullingstone Roman Villa (2) turn left on a footpath that rises among trees. Emerging from the little woodland the way continues to climb, enclosed between a hedge and a wire fence. On the way to the crown of the slope ignore alternative paths to right and left. Through the hedge and trees on the left can be seen some fine distant views.

From the crown of the hill huge views overlook the Darent Valley and out to the south where the Greensand Ridge blocks the horizon. Ahead can be heard the drone of traffic on the M25. The path brings you to a gap in a long line of trees where other paths converge (GR: 522655). Go through the gap and turn left to walk along the edge of a large field.

At the end of this field one line of trees goes off to the right, with another ahead. Go straight ahead along a footpath with a coomb folding to the left where a golf course may be seen. Come to a field gate with a stile next to it, and maintain direction on a clear track that passes through more gates, goes beyond some farm buildings and eventually reaches Lullingstone Park (3).

Turn left and walk through the car park to the far right-hand corner where a surfaced track leads into the Park; the golf course stretches far ahead and there's a picnic area on the right. Wander along the track for about 120 yards, then head off to the right where a signpost directs the way to a 'Woodland Walk'. There is no footpath on the ground, but you simply make towards a marker post seen at an obvious gap in the woods. Cross by a golf course tee and enter Beechen Wood on a clear track sloping down. At the foot of the slope emerge from the trees to cross a fairway (beware flying golf balls).

Walk ahead to the grassy slope opposite, and a few yards up this slant half-left on a continuing path going uphill in the woods. At the top of the slope come to cross-tracks. Continue ahead, over a stile next to a ladder stile, and along an enclosed footpath which leads to a field. Cross this to Redmans Lane (GR: 510637) where you turn left, and in about 100 yards bear right on a concrete driveway. Wander along this, then on the path at its end to pass two bungalows. At the end of the second garden fence the path bears right to enter a large field.

Follow the right-hand edge to its far corner and cross a stile into a sloping meadow. There are some lovely views at this point, out to the steep scarp slope of the North Downs on the far side of the valley. Hills of woodland and meadow fold into green vales ahead.

Descend the scrub-pocked meadow to the far left-hand corner where a stile brings you onto a lane opposite a cottage (GR: 514628). Bear left, following the lane through an avenue of mature trees. Turn right at a T junction and in a few paces note some steps on the right which lead to an interesting memorial stone. Continue along the lane, walking uphill to another junction. Ignore the left turn to Shoreham and stay on the right fork, but on reaching a cottage standing beside the lane, turn along a track immediately on the left of the driveway. (This track runs above and to the right of a sunken pathway.) The track veers to the right and rises steadily before coming to a fork by a sign announcing Meenfield Wood. Continue straight ahead on the left-hand option; steep meadows fall away to the left.

The way passes above a large memorial cross cut into the chalk slope, and soon after comes to a crossing path. Turn left and descend towards Shoreham (4). The path becomes enclosed and leads into Shoreham High Street where you turn right, then take the first road left into Church Street.

Down Church Street pass the weatherboarded Kings Arms with its unusual ostler's box, then cross the Darent over an attractive bridge. Bear left, pass the village war memorial and walk ahead towards the entrance to The Water House where Samuel Palmer, the artist once lived. Veer left on a surfaced path that follows the stream, and when a footbridge allows cross to the left bank. The continuing route is waymarked for the Darent Valley Path. It comes to a lane, curves right and continues as a footpath along the left bank of the Darent before entering a large field. Walk along the right headland as the stream winds away. At the end of the field the Darent has found its way back again, but once more the path deserts it and crosses the centre of the next field. On the far side go over a concrete farm road and continue ahead along the left-hand side of a hop garden, joining a country road by some houses.

Wander ahead along this road to reach Lullingstone Park Visitor Centre.

Items of interest:

1: Lullingstone Castle. Not a castle at all, but a Tudor mansion hidden behind a red-brick Queen Anne façade. The home for many generations of the Hart-Dyke family, a small flint chapel in the grounds contains the effigies of a large number of them. The Castle is open to the public on set days during the summer.

2: Lullingstone Roman Villa. In the third century A.D. a small villa-cum-farmhouse was built on the fertile meadows of the Darent's left bank by a Roman farmer. It was later enlarged to house an important official, and superb mosaic floors were laid out. There were baths and under-floor heating and, perhaps surprisingly, a Christian chapel. The remains of this villa are now open to the public and well worth a visit.

3: Lullingstone Park. Created by Sevenoaks District Council the Park consists of about 300 acres of parkland and woods in which there is a golf course, a picnic area and a nature trail. The bar and restaurant at the golf course entrance is open to the public. The Visitor Centre has interpretive displays, a cafeteria, and local books and walks leaflets for sale.

4: Shoreham. This surprisingly unspoilt village is one of the most attractive in the Darent Valley, with its tile-hung or flint-walled cottages, several pubs, a lovely church and picturesque bridge over the stream. Its most famous resident was Samuel Palmer, the landscape artist (1805-1881), who lived here for about seven years. Of those years he wrote: "Everything connected with the village in those happy times seemed wrapped about with a sentiment of cosy quiet antiquity, full of association that carried you back into the pastoral life of Merry England years ago."

WALK 3: KEMSING - ASHDOWN FARM - KEMSING

Distance:	3 miles
Maps:	O.S. Pathfinder 1208 'Sevenoaks & Westerham' 1:25,000
	O.S. Landranger 188 'Maidstone & The Weald of Kent' 1:50,000
Start:	Kemsing Village Hall (GR: 555586)
Access:	East of A225 near Otford Station, a narrow road (The Pilgrims Way) is signposted to Kemsing. The hall stands in the heart of the village not far from the church. Nearest railway stations: Kemsing and Otford
Parking:	Behind Kemsing Village Hall, next to The Wheatsheaf pub
Refreshments:	Pubs in Kemsing and opposite Ashdown Farm

To the north of Sevenoaks, hemmed in between motorway and downs, sprawls the commuter village of Kemsing. Immediately behind it the North Downs form a steep and imposing wall, while between the village and the downs runs The Pilgrims Way. Along the upper slopes of Green Hill above the church and youth hostel, the trail of the North Downs Way follows a scenic course. Up there, with enormous views, one's gaze sweeps across Kemsing, Seal, Otford and Sevenoaks to the damaged tree-cluster of the greensand hills. Long vistas reveal the line of the downs to east and west; a long blue line with its jutting prows and curving coombs creating individual features. On the cropped slopes wild flowers star the grass, while among the trees traveller's joy (wild clematis, or old man's beard) clambers with unrestrained vigour.

This short, but fairly energetic, walk ascends the scarp slope to Green Hill, then makes a traverse of the upper hillside, and alongside spring-crazy bluebell woods, over meadows and through spinneys in the North Downs 'back country'. It visits a remote pub, and then returns to Kemsing by way of more woods on the downland rim before swooping down to the valley again.

Views will be memorable, and as there are plenty of idyllic picnic sites along the way, it would be worth making this a longer day's outing than the modest distance might otherwise suggest. Be tempted. Take a packed lunch and enjoy the great expanse of open sky and unchecked vista - and listen to the songs of the birds.

*   *   *

At the rear of the car park, beside a lamp standard, there's access to a footpath which goes round to the church. But instead of following this to the right, go straight ahead along an alternative path. On coming to a brick wall bear right and continue, passing between the village school and the youth hostel, and soon come to the narrow lane of The Pilgrims Way. Cross over to the steep downland slope of Green Hill.

Climb straight ahead. There is no real footpath, but you simply stagger up and up towards trees at the head of the slope. As you draw near to them you will notice half-left ahead, the imposing Hildenborough Hall. A convenient seat has been placed near the crown of the hill from which to enjoy magnificent views of the surrounding countryside.

A clear path projects beyond the seat and goes into woodland clothing the upper slopes. Before long cross a stile, and when the path forks soon after, take the left-hand option. This leads across an open stretch of downland below Hildenborough Hall, and on the far side joins the route of the North Downs Way. Keep ahead along

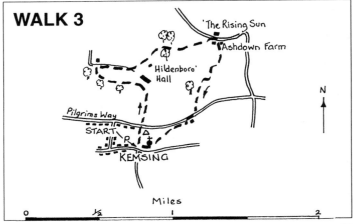

this through trees and scrub, with views into the valley marked by the gleam of water at Chipstead Lakes (1).

Another stile takes the path onto Whiteleaf Down, more heavily wooded than before, and eventually comes to a bench seat with another fine view. Here the North Downs Way climbs to the right, among trees of a Nature Reserve, then follows along the edge of woodland, still gaining height. At last come to a narrow lane opposite a thatched cottage (GR: 551596). Turn right and passing through a large gateway (the entrance to the driveway of Hildenborough Hall) wander down the drive.

The driveway is bordered by a trim hedge. When it finishes cross a stile on the left, and immediately bear right to continue in the same direction. At the end of the first field come to a woodland shaw, cross a stile and bear half-left to walk across the next field aiming well to the left of a solitary cottage seen on the far side. Come to a stile leading into another field, and maintain direction towards Fab's Wood. There you will see two footpaths. Take the right-hand option through the wood.

Emerging from the trees cross a field, slightly to the left, aiming more or less towards the roof of a bungalow that can be seen a couple of fields away. Just to the left of some holly bushes growing beneath a large oak tree, cross another stile and walk down the right-hand side of the next field. This brings you to an enclosed footpath leading to a narrow country lane. Turn right, and in a few paces reach The Rising Sun pub (GR: 563599), a typical downland building of flint construction set, it would seem, a long way from anywhere.

Opposite the pub turn right on another enclosed footpath by the entrance to Ashdown Farm. Along this path you pass a little duckpond. Reaching the corner of a wood cross a stile and continue ahead with the woodland to your right, then reach another stile. Enter the wood and rejoin the North Downs Way - but only for a short distance. On coming to yet another stile, this time on the left, cross and go down the edge of a sloping field, at the bottom of which turn right and keep to the boundary until you come to another stile on the left. The path now goes through a woodland shaw, beyond which bear right across the corner of another sloping meadow to find yet one more stile leading into woods again. The path now winds downhill, soon becomes enclosed by high fences, and discharges onto The Pilgrims Way.

Turn right, and after passing the first cottage on the left take to the path beside it, then immediately bear right on a footpath which leads along the top edge of a large sports field. When you can see a children's play area in the bottom corner, cut down towards it, then leave by way of a gate near the church. Enter Kemsing (2) churchyard through the lych gate and follow the left-hand path which leads to the village car park.

Items of interest:

1: Chipstead Lakes. Seen in the distance, these flooded one-time gravel pits have been adopted as a wildfowl reserve.

2: Kemsing. Although the village is dominated by commuter sprawl, it retains a neat and historic heart. The church of St Mary is lovingly treasured; a place of calm that holds something of almost every age since the Normans. Behind it, in what was formerly the Vicarage, stands the youth hostel. In the village street there are trim cottages and, by the war memorial, a little sunken garden containing St Edith's Well. A spring gushes freely with its power, so we are told, to cure sore eyes. The view from Green Hill above the village will do that too.

WALK 4: TROSLEY COUNTRY PARK - TROTTISCLIFFE CHURCH - TROSLEY

Distance:	3¹/₂ miles
Maps:	O.S. Pathfinder 1193 'Chatham' 1:25,000
	O.S. Landranger 188 'Maidstone & The Weald of Kent' 1:50,000
Start:	Trosley Country Park (GR: 635612)
Access:	Signposted from A227 Wrotham-Gravesend road, about 2 miles north-east of Wrotham
Parking:	At Trosley Country Park (small charge made)
Refreshments:	None

Trosley Country Park covers 160 acres of mature woods and scrub downland on the very lip of the North Downs, from which some of Kent's broadest panoramas may be enjoyed. Within the Park there's a large car park, picnic area, public toilets, information boards and a Visitor Centre open at weekends and bank holidays. Circular walks have been waymarked, and the North Downs Way passes through.

The following route is a shortened version of Walk 5, but although it covers only a modest distance, it rewards with plenty of interest and some delightful views. The church at Trottiscliffe (pronounced Trosley) is worth visiting, and not simply for its architecture and fitments. Set among farm buildings it is the epitome of rural worship. Not far away the Coldrum Long Barrow is worth a short diversion. But it is the huge panoramas that stay longest in mind. Ever-changing, yet always magnificent, they demand constant halts for contemplation and photography.

As the Park gates are locked at dusk it is important to return to your vehicle before this time.

* * *

Just below the Visitor Centre descend to a broad crossing track (the North Downs Way) and bear left. After about 300 yards turn right at a marker post and go down a series of steps through the woods. At the foot of the tree-clad slope bear left beside a wire fence. Some 300 yards later another marker post sends you to the right, across a bridleway and between wooden barriers onto a narrow country

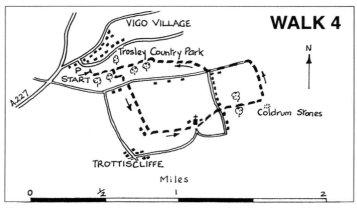

road - The Pilgrims Way (GR: 639610). Crossing this go through a swing gate into a meadow and walk straight ahead down its right-hand boundary. Trottiscliffe church can be seen tucked in its hollow among farm buildings a couple of fields away.

Continue in the same direction, eventually passing along the end of some gardens beyond which you come to a crossing path. Turn left here and wander ahead to the farmyard of Court Lodge Farm. A few paces beyond this stands the church of St Peter and St Paul (1). It's a lovely church and worth spending a few minutes inside. Sit in one of the pews and absorb the mystery of rural peace, and think of the day's gifts. There are more to come.

Beyond the church pass an attractive 18th-century house and go up a footpath on the left. Halfway up the slope pause to study the group of church, houses and farm buildings below. The path continues along the edge of a large field and comes to Pinesfield Lane opposite a long row of bungalows. Cross the lane and wander along a track signposted to Coldrum Long Barrow. This track leads through a scrubby patch of woodland, and along the edge of a field. On the far side come onto a crossing track.

Note: To visit the Coldrum Long Barrow (or Coldrum Stones), bear right here and walk a short distance to find the remains of this Neolithic burial chamber behind a wooden fence. For details, see Walk 5.

To continue with the walk bear left along a footpath used by the Wealdway (2) which heads towards the North Downs. It brings you to the lane of The Pilgrims Way once more, where you turn left for about 500 yards. Drawing level with the end of Pinesfield Lane (GR: 648612), leave The Pilgrims Way and go through a gate on the right to re-enter Trosley Country Park (3). In a few paces bear left to pass below a one-time chalk quarry, and begin to climb the slope with fine views again down to Trottiscliffe church and out to the broad acres of the Weald.

The way continues to angle up the hillside, passing through two or three gates with views becoming more expansive as you gain height. After a while wander through an area of mature yew trees, some of which were felled by the '87 storm. The path twists a little to the left and descends some steps before veering right again. Emerge from the woods to a more open hillside and continue ahead, climbing again with lovely views of the downs and the valley. Then up another flight of steps to gain a broad crossing track where you turn left and walk back to the Visitor Centre and car park.

Items of interest:

1: Trottiscliffe church. The church of St Peter and St Paul, Trottiscliffe, is delightfully set among farm buildings below the steep scarp slope of the downs. It's a simple, historic church with a flint-studded tower and sarsen stones in its foundations, said to have been built by William the Conqueror's Bishop Gundulph in 1100 on the site of an earlier Saxon place of worship. Go inside and listen to the centuries whispering. In this compact place of peace and hope there are dark box pews and a pulpit brought from Westminster Abbey in 1824 without prior consent of the Dean and Chapter.

2: The Wealdway. This long-distance trail is met on several walks included in this book. It links Gravesend on the Thames with Beachy Head near Eastbourne; 82 miles of footpaths, tracks and country lanes that explore some surprisingly remote countryside. Guidebook: *The Wealdway & The Vanguard Way* by Kev Reynolds (Cicerone Press).

3: Trosley Country Park. Established by the Amenities and Countryside Committee of Kent County Council, the 160 acres of woods and downland make a splendid base for a day's walking. Although the '87 storm felled a number of fine mature trees, the woods are re-establishing themselves, and where gaps in the tree cover have been made, visitors are now able to enjoy views previously denied them. Publications on sale at the Visitor Centre include *Exploring Trosley Country Park* (an education pack related to the National Curriculum for Primary age children), and *Trosley Country Park Wildlife Walks* - walks, wildlife and general information.

WALK 5: TROSLEY COUNTRY PARK - COLDRUM STONES - CONEY LODGE FARM - TROSLEY

Distance:	6 miles
Maps:	O.S. Pathfinder 1193 'Chatham' 1:25,000
	O.S. Landranger 188 'Maidstone & The Weald of Kent' 1:50,000
Start:	Trosley Country Park (GR: 635612)
Access:	Signposted from A227 Wrotham-Gravesend road, about 2 miles north-east of Wrotham
Parking:	At Trosley Country Park (small charge made)
Refreshments:	None

This, the second of our walks from Trosley Country Park, is an extension of Walk 4. It enjoys all the features of that previous walk, but has the additional pleasure of exploring more woodland and open field scenery below the downs, as well as making a point of visiting the Coldrum Stones, or Coldrum Long Barrow - one of several prehistoric sites set on or below the North Downs on either side of the Medway Gap.

* * *

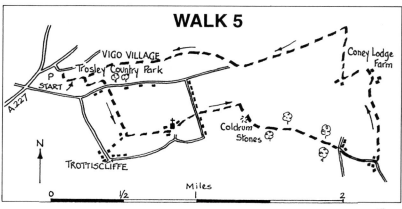

On leaving the car park and Visitor Centre at Trosley, follow directions as for Walk 4 beyond Trottiscliffe church and as far as the Coldrum Long Barrow (1) - (GR: 654607).With the Long Barrow on your right walk along a concrete farm road for a few yards until it curves to the right, then leave it to go straight ahead on a broad track towards the corner of a woodland (Wealdway waymarks). At the left-hand corner you will find a pair of stiles. Leaving the route of the Wealdway here cross the first of these and go along the left-hand edge of a field. When the field cuts back, continue ahead to enter a wood whose footpath route through is often very muddy after rain.

Emerging from the wood cross a stile into a fenced meadow and aim for the far-right corner where another stile takes the path into an area of replanted woodland. Again, the path is often muddy as you enter, but it improves as you walk up the slope. On the far side come to a country lane opposite some cottages (GR: 665604).

Bear right, then almost immediately take the left fork and wander down the road for about a third of a mile, towards the village of Ryarsh seen ahead with the M20 motorway beyond it. The road curves to the right between houses. Pass the first house on the left, then bear left along the end of some gardens. The path now swings left into fields and you continue ahead in the same direction, soon beside a little brook, alongside a woodland, then across a field towards another woodland. Here the path bears right, then left through a gap, and right to farm buildings and a concrete farm road.

Turn left and walk on to the red-brick Coney Lodge Farm at a T junction of farm roads (GR: 667613). Turn left again and continue towards Park Farm. Just short of the farm turn right along an enclosed bridleway heading towards the North Downs. (An alternative footpath here cuts through the left-hand field and rejoins our route later on The Pilgrims Way.) The bridleway becomes a narrow sunken track, and leads directly to a major crossing track which is the route of both The Pilgrims Way and North Downs Way. Bear left along it for a little under a mile until the track becomes a narrow metalled lane. Now turn right between houses and go steeply up the downland slope among heavy yew trees. Near the head of the slope bear sharp left, go through a gate and re-enter Trosley Country Park. Simply follow the main trail all the way to the car park.

Items of interest:

1: Coldrum Long Barrow. Also known as the Coldrum Stones, this important Neolithic site is held in the care of the National Trust and is accessible at all times. What we see are the remains of a complex burial chamber raised some 4,000-5,000 years ago; massive sarsen stones (slabs of crystalline sandstone), many of which have collapsed in a rough circle measuring 160 feet in circumference. Originally they would have stood upright - four of the 24 columns still do - with a huge covering mound of earth, and with only the entrance kept clear. They form one of the locations of a series of Neolithic sites representative of what is now known as the 'Medway Culture'. Others nearby include Addington, and Kits Coty above Aylesford on the right bank of the Medway. It is assumed they would have been linked by ancient trackways that are today followed by the route of the North Downs Way.

WALK 6: HOLLY HILL - LUDDESDOWN - HOLLY HILL

Distance:	4^1/$_2$ miles
Maps:	O.S. Pathfinder 1193 'Chatham' 1:25,000
	O.S. Landranger 177 'East London Area' or 178 'The Thames Estuary' 1:50,000
Start:	Holly Hill car park (GR: 670629)
Access:	Turn off A227 Wrotham-Gravesend road about 2 miles north-east of Wrotham, heading east for about 2^1/$_2$ miles (passing Vigo village). At Birling Hill a sudden view is afforded to the right. Turn left on a no-through-road which leads in ^{1}/$_2$ mile to Holly Hill car park
Parking:	Free parking at Holly Hill
Refreshments:	None

As one of the highest points on the North Downs, Holly Hill enjoys spectacular views: eastward over the Medway Valley, north through the deep cut of a valley leading to Luddesdown and, from the southern edge at Birling Hill, a magnificent vista overlooking the immense spread of the northern Weald. It's good walking country too, with short circular walks

47

and several long-distance trails passing through.

This route takes us into a seemingly secret, forgotten landscape. Yet the Medway Towns to the east, and Gravesend to the north, are never far away, although their proximity has made no great impact on the countryside here. Between Holly Hill and the ancient hamlet of Luddesdown rolls a land as remote and peaceful as any walker in lowland England might expect to find.

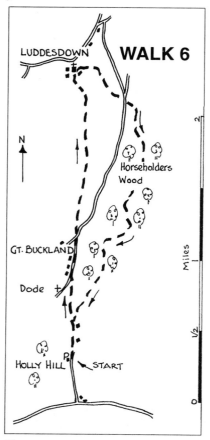

*   *   *

Leave the car park and turn left along the narrow lane which at this point is part of the North Downs Way (1). Ignore the drive forking right and continue, passing a farmyard, then Holly Hill House, beyond which the road becomes a track. When it curves off to the right, leave it (and the North Downs Way) and go straight ahead, now on a more narrow track descending through woodland. Cut deeply by the rains of many decades the track carves its way between storm-ravaged woods through which a soft light hints of distant views. At the foot of the slope turn right on a very narrow lane (GR: 669637).

Note: A short diversion left will bring you to the sad, isolated little church of Dode (2) whose congregation died out in the 14th century with the

Black Death.

Swinging down the lane pass the few farms and houses that make up the hamlet of Great Buckland. On either side wooded spurs of the North Downs contain a peaceful valley. Soon come to a junction of lanes. Directly ahead will be seen a footpath sign beside a telegraph pole, and a stile leading into a large field. Here you join the Wealdway.

Walk ahead through the field in a scoop of valley known as the Bowling Alley. The route is clearly waymarked and straightforward. It crosses several stiles and, from the top of a rise, provides a good view onto Luddesdown (3), its farm, church and curious architectural style of a house near the church. Ignore alternative paths and go down the slope on the right-hand edge of a meadow towards farm buildings. Come onto a farm road, bear right and in a few paces reach Luddesdown church.

Departing from the Wealdway now, pass the church on your left and one or two houses and a lovely thatched barn on the right, and come to a gateway. Bear right on a footpath down a slope beside a hedge. Over a stile follow the headland of a field for about 120 yards, then go uphill through a little woodland shaw. Out of the trees bear right along the edge of a field, ignoring another path off to the left. When the hedge ends continue ahead to reach a junction of narrow country roads (GR:675658).

Cross and go uphill on an enclosed bridleway. When it forks continue ahead on what is the left branch. The way continues to climb, still enclosed by trees and hedges, but becomes a pretence of a belvedere with hinted views to the tree-capped hills beyond the Bowling Alley.

Eventually veer slightly left out of the trees and continue alongside a field. Maintaining direction enter Horseholders Wood. The track, cut and churned by numerous horses' hooves, provides one suggestion as to why it is so-named. The trail veers to the right through a field gate, and then along a fairly straight and level 'ride'. This leads to the edge of the woods at an enclosed field with power lines marching across it. The track forks. Take the left-hand option. At the end of the wood it is joined by a second track. Go ahead for a few yards, under power lines, then turn right on the North Downs Way. Going through a gap with a marker post the path goes to the right of the hedge in front of you, slants across the field beneath another string of power cables, and makes for a line of trees in the far left-hand corner of the field.

At a choice of paths take that which is ahead and leading slightly to the left. A North Downs Way acorn symbol is your marker here. The path leads through a scrubby woodland at first, but then a more mature assortment of beech, oak and yew take over. Come to a wooden fence where the path bears round to the right. This soon becomes more of a track that should be familiar as it is the outward track from Holly Hill. (The left-hand fence marks the boundary to Holly Hill House.) The way leads to a road which takes you back to the car park.

Items of interest:

1: The North Downs Way. One of the oldest of our National Trails, the North Downs Way is 141 miles long, and leads from Farnham in Surrey to Dover, with a secondary spur to Canterbury. Plenty of attractive country is explored on this route, and several walks in this guidebook share sections of the Way. There are several guidebooks to this long-distance trail, perhaps the best being: *A Guide to the Pilgrims Way and North Downs Way* by Christopher John Wright (Constable).

2: Dode church. A tiny deserted Norman church, barn-like in appearance, it was originally thatched but was tiled during restoration work carried out in 1905-06. The community it served was decimated by the Black Death of 1349.

3: Luddesdown. The history of this tiny hamlet goes back to Stone Age times. Signs of dwellings of both Stone Age and Iron Age man have been discovered here. Roman pottery has been picked up on the slopes above, and there are Roman tiles set in the lower walls of the church. In Saxon times King Harold's brother, Lewin, was lord of the manor, presumably living in what is today Luddesdown Court next to the church. This house has been continuously lived in for at least 900 years, for on the death of Harold at Hastings it was taken over by Bishop Odo, who came ashore with William the Conqueror. The house is not open to the public.

WALK 7: HOLLY HILL - COLDRUM STONES - HOLLY HILL

Distance:	5$^{1}/_{2}$ miles
Maps:	O.S. Pathfinder 1193 'Chatham' 1:25,000
	O.S. Landranger 178 'The Thames Estuary' or 188 'Maidstone & The Weald of Kent' 1:50,000
Start:	Holly Hill car park (GR: 670629)
Access:	Turn off A227 Wrotham-Gravesend road about 2 miles north-east of Wrotham, heading east for about 2$^{1}/_{2}$ miles (passing Vigo village). At Birling Hill a sudden view is afforded to the right. Turn left on a no-through-road which leads in $^{1}/_{2}$ mile to Holly Hill car park.
Parking:	Free parking at Holly Hill
Refreshments:	None

While Walk 6 explored the inner downs north of Holly Hill, this route takes in the steep scarp slope to the south, with those enormous views spread before us. The outing encompasses woodland and downland meadow, steep slopes and low-lying field paths. It goes along the North Downs Way, touches the Pilgrims Way, and shares for a brief spell the path of the Wealdway. It also follows a section of Walk 5 (which begins at Trosley Country Park), but as well as combining many other recreational trails, it does make the most of age-old field trails that owe their existence - as do most footpaths elsewhere in this book - to the passage of country folk going about their daily business for many generations.

In addition to the glorious views, added interest is provided by a visit to the Coldrum Stones. On the site of this Neolithic long barrow have been found either skeletons or other remains of 22 people, as well as the bones of various animals. In 1926 the Coldrum Stones were handed into the care of the National Trust in memory of Ightham grocer and inspired archaeologist, Benjamin Harrison, who became widely renowned for his work in the locality. (See also notes on the Oldbury Hill Walk 13.)

*   *   *

On entry to the unmade car park at Holly Hill you will notice a track leading into the woods at the far right-hand corner. Walk along this, skirting the woodland edge with fields to your right, soon with views into a tight little valley that leads to Luddesdown. The track descends and swings leftward into the woods which offer a mass of bluebells in springtime. Continue along this main track, ignoring alternatives to right and left, and eventually come to a narrow country road next to the flint-and brick-built Harvel Lodge (GR: 665623).

Bear right for a few paces, then left into Whitehorse Wood on a bridleway. As is the nature of such bridleways it is often muddy. Soon reach the lip of the downs to be treated to a wide and wonderful view of the Weald framed by trees. On this edge of the scarp slope there's a junction of tracks. Stay with the main track as it swings slightly to the right and begins to descend the hillside.

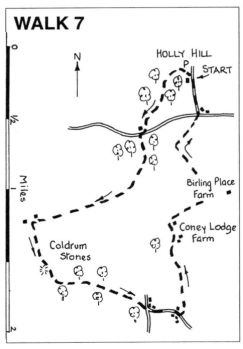

Between trees the Medway can be seen winding through the valley, with the eastern extension of the North Downs making a distant wall of blue to contain the countless acres of the Weald. An enormous view. On the descent the track enters what is almost a tunnel formed by the intertwining of yew and beech trees; enclosures of cool air on a warm summer's day.

Near the foot of the slope turn right along the North Downs Way, which you follow for about

³/₄ mile to a very narrow metalled lane (The Pilgrims Way) near an attractive white timber-framed cottage. Almost immediately turn left on a clear path signposted to the Coldrum Long Barrow. Walking along this path, which is shared with the Wealdway, there are more big views to enjoy across the Medway Gap to the continuing downs. Come to a concrete farm road and a few paces later you will see the Coldrum Long Barrow (1) on the right behind a wooden fence (GR: 654607). It is worth a few minutes of study; there is an explanatory board by the surrounding fence, and a walkway round the site.

Continue along the farm road until it curves to the right. Leave it here and walk ahead on a broad track into a corner of Ryarsh Wood. On coming to two stiles cross the first and walk down the side of a field alongside a woodland shaw. When the field cuts off to the left continue ahead, over a stile on the far side and through another wood on a rather muddy path. Reaching a fenced meadow cross another stile and walk across to the far right-hand corner, and there enter a replanted area of woodland. At first the path may be very sticky, but it improves as you walk up the gentle slope. The path emerges onto a country road opposite some cottages (GR: 665604).

Turn right and almost immediately fork left. Walk down the road for about a third of a mile with the village of Ryarsh seen ahead, with the M20 motorway beyond - its constant drone a reminder of the peace temporarily forsaken. The road curves right between houses. Immediately past the first house on the left, bear left along the bottom of some gardens. The footpath swings left into a field where you walk straight ahead, then alongside a little brook, beside a woodland and across a field towards another wood. Here the path bears right, then left through a gap, and right again to a farm drive by some large barns (GR: 668611).

Turn left along the concrete drive, and when you reach the red-brick Coney Lodge Farm at a T junction of farm roads, bear right between large open fields. Passing a black barn the road begins to rise, and at the top of the slope, just short of Birling Place, turn left along a track towards the North Downs. At cross-tracks rejoin the North Downs Way; go ahead, over a stile and along an enclosed path to the very foot of the downs. Another stile directs you to the right along the tree- and scrub-covered slope, then on a stiff climb up the flank of the North Downs, with views growing as you gain height.

At the head of the slope come onto a narrow road at Birling Hill opposite Holly Hill Lodge. Wander ahead along the no-through-road which leads directly to the car park at Holly Hill (2).

Items of interest:

1: The Coldrum Long Barrow. Also known as the Coldrum Stones, this is one of several important Neolithic sites grouped in this corner of the county as part of the so-called 'Medway Culture'. Dating between 2,000 and 3,000 B.C., the Long Barrow was a complex burial chamber consisting of 24 columns of sarsen stones gathered in a large circle, then covered by a huge mound of earth with only the entrance kept clear. Only four of the original columns are left standing, the remainder lying where they fell. The site, given to the National Trust in 1926, has revealed a number of human remains as well as various animal bones.

2: Holly Hill. One of Kent's Public Open Spaces, Holly Hill consists of 32 acres of woodland, with views across the Medway Valley.

WALK 8: CAMER COUNTRY PARK - COBHAM - LUDDESDOWN - CAMER COUNTRY PARK

Distance:	5 miles
Maps:	O.S. Pathfinder 1193 'Chatham' 1:25,000
	O.S. Landranger 177 'East London Area' or 178 'The Thames Estuary' 1:50,000
Start:	Camer Country Park (GR: 650669)
Access:	Via B2009 north-east of Meopham. Park entrance off Camer Park Road. Nearest railway station: Sole Street
Parking:	Camer Country Park
Refreshments:	Pubs at Sole Street and Cobham

Camer Country Park is a delightful 45 acre parkland site just over a mile from Meopham. Gravesend is less than 5 miles away, and Rochester not much more than that. Camer is set in gentle countryside, with no shortage of pleasant circular walks possible from it. This is just one possibility, a walk that explores acres and acres of orchards, big flat fields and plunging downland slopes, neat valleys and jackdaw-loud woods. Tiny hamlets lie hidden in folding coombs sliced through the chalk, bearing in their walls and in their neat thatched hills a thousand years and more of history.

Footpaths used on this walk are popular with local ramblers, and two long-distance trails that pass through (the Wealdway and London Countryway) introduce walkers from farther afield too to some of the pleasures of the North Downs heartland. Paths and waymarks are in better condition than in many other areas, but with so many paths to choose from it's necessary to keep alert at junctions.

*   *   *

Enter the Park by way of Camer Park Road and walk ahead along the left-hand boundary (stately trees and a great sweep of trim grass), and exit beside East Lodge to come onto the B2009. Continue ahead on the pavement towards The Railway Inn, then bear right

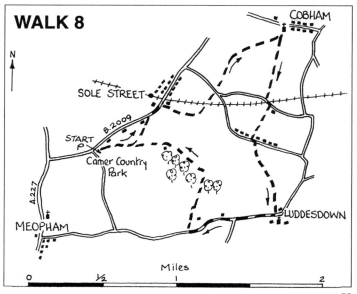

opposite the pub on an enclosed footpath signposted to Little Buckland and Luddesdown. On coming to a large field take the path heading half-left across it parallel with the railway. The wide open landscape is spoilt only by a marching line of silver pylons carrying overhead power cables. Larks rise singing, tiny specks of magic in a huge sky.

Halfway across draw level with a footbridge over the railway. Bear left on a crossing path, go over the bridge and continue, now a little to the right and come to a country lane. Go straight over and into a large orchard. Bear right, then left between orchards on a vague track for a few hundred yards. The way then veers a little to the right, and passing beneath three lines of overhead cables continues towards Cobham church. All around lies a vast acreage of orchards - hundreds and hundreds of fruit trees marching in regimental rows across the countryside.

Come to a stile in a hedge and enter Cobham churchyard. In a few paces another footpath breaks off to the right. This is the one to take. But before doing so it is worth making a short diversion to visit Cobham (1), an interesting village with Dickens connections, a church with a notable collection of brasses, and behind it a most attractive quadrangle of almshouses. (To visit the village continue ahead through the churchyard to the main street. Bear right for shops, pubs and public toilets.)

Resuming the walk bear right through the graveyard extension and exit by a stile. The continuing footpath goes along the right-hand edge of a large field. On the far side come to a narrow country lane by a railway bridge (GR: 668676). Cross the bridge, and shortly after turn right just before a grey house. The path goes alongside the boundary hedge, then you cross a stile and go over a small paddock, through a swing gate and down to the houses of Henley Street seen below. Wandering between gardens you come to a lane which runs from Sole Street to Luddesdown (GR: 667672).

Turn left along the lane for a few paces, then cross a stile on the right into a sloping field. Go up this aiming half-left to a woodland shaw. The path continues to climb through the short, but steep shaw, and out at the corner of a large open field. This is Henley Down. Continue straight across it, over the brow of the hill where a 360 degree panorama gives a landscape of folding hills and gentle

Cobham College and church - sun-warmed stone on the North Downs

valleys, all spread beneath a vast umbrella sky. To the south the downs pour into a hinted vale where a huddle of buildings is your first sight of Luddesdown (2). Behind that the hills climb once more in an arc of woodland.

On the far side of the field go through a narrow patch of scrubby trees and bushes, and onto the upper edge of a steep field above Luddesdown. Plunge down the slope towards the right-hand edge of a circular greensward - Luddesdown's cricket pitch - and on to a lane by the village hall. Beyond that stands the church.

Turn right and walk along the lane away from Luddesdown church for about ³/₄ mile; a pleasant stroll among trees with jackdaws cawing and scrapping in the uppermost branches overhead, and with a line of hills curving to the right. Another lane comes in from the left, and shortly after this you pass a farm on the right with a number of stables - there are often many horses grazing the surrounding meadows. The lane drops into a hollow and climbs out the other side. Passing the entrance to Bramble Hall Farm continue for a further 250 yards, then cross a stile on the right, marked by a signpost to Sole Street and Henley Street.

Go up a slope of meadowland towards the top right-hand corner where another stile leads into Henley Wood. A clear footpath leads through, and soon brings you to a junction of trails. Bear slightly left on the main path which continues through the wood, then out to the corner of a field (GR: 661665). Maintain direction along the left-hand edge of the field beside the continuing woodland. At the far side come to a junction of four paths. Bear left on the route of the Wealdway, still beside Henley Wood. The rooftops of Henley Street can be seen down in the dip to the right, with Cobham church tower in the distance.

Come to another junction of tracks where the field makes a half-corner. Bear half-right on a track which soon passes an isolated house, then edges a large field all the way to the B2009 beside East Lodge. Before reaching that, however, where the track makes a sharp right-hand bend, enter Camer Country Park (3) by a gate on the left.

Items of interest:

1: Cobham. The village contains much of interest. First the church of St Mary Magdalene, noted for having some of the finest brasses in England; there's a veritable gallery of them spread along the chancel floor below the altar. Behind the church the ragstone almshouses of Cobham College stand in a trim rectangle, which is open to the public at set times. In the village street, right opposite the church, stands The Leather Bottle Inn, a sizeable half-timbered coaching inn which featured in Dickens' *The Pickwick Papers*. The novelist's portrait is incorporated in the Inn's sign. Dickens lived nearby, at Gad's Hill, and often walked the footpaths round here. A short distance along the village street to the left is Owletts, a red-brick 17th-century house with a fine staircase and formal gardens. In the hands of the National Trust it is open to the public. To the east of the village is one of Dickens' favourite places: Cobham Hall. He described it as: "an ancient hall displaying the quaint and picturesque architecture of Elizabeth's time". Dickens often walked from his home at Gad's Hill to the great park which surrounds Cobham Hall, a lavish 16th-century mansion now housing a girls' school, but open to the public during school holidays.

2: Luddesdown. This tiny but historic hamlet dates back to the Stone Age. There were settlements here in both Stone Age and Iron Age times, and the Romans must have been here too, for there are Roman tiles set in the walls of the church. Lewin, brother to King Harold who lost his kingdom (as well as his eye) at Hastings, once was lord of the manor, but it passed to Bishop Odo who came over with the Conqueror. He lived at what is now Luddesdown Court beside the church; the house has been lived in continuously since then.

3: Camer Country Park. Owned and managed by Gravesham District Council, the Park was established in 1971. It comprises 45 acres of parkland and fine trees. There's free car parking, an adventure playground, and public toilets. *Camer Country Park - Circular Walks from Country Parks* describes three circular walks of 3-4 miles starting from the Park.

The Greensand Hills

The hills of the Lower Greensand form a parallel ridge to the line of
the North Downs, but they are different in structure to the downs,
different in character, yet their imposition on the landscape remains
every bit as powerful as that of the downs. "Ah, the Kentish Alps!"
exclaimed a Swiss friend one day as we journeyed north through the
valley of the Eden and gazed at the undulating ridge ahead where
Mariners Hill, Toys Hill and the double horns of Ide Hill emerged
from a skein of autumn mist.

It's all fine walking country. The soil, consisting more of sand
than of downland chalk, encourages a lush vegetation cover that
contrasts with that of the North Downs. There are pine woods, and
chestnut, birch and beech trees crown the hills. Between them small
heathlands are sometimes to be found, with bracken and heather
and bilberry fighting for supremacy. There are jungles of
rhododendron to bring colour blazing from the hills in May and
June, while in springtime an abundance of wild flowers are there to
be enjoyed on hilltop and in sheltered valley. Towards Maidstone,
beyond the Medway, sunny slopes are clothed with great orchards
of apple and cherry, and tilted fields striped with currant bushes
and soft fruits stretch in rows by the acre above the Weald.

For much of the Greensand Ridge a distinct escarpment breaks
dramatically on its southern edge. In the western end of the county,
where it enters from Surrey, the scarp slope has suffered the
upheaval of landslip from time to time. In 1596, for example, at
Froghole near Crockham Hill, springs had so undermined the
hillside that over a period of eleven days the slope of meadowland
between Froghole and Crockham Hill church dragged trees and
hedges and deposited them in newly formed hollows. Hills arose
where there had been no hills before, and ponds were formed on
previously dry ground. The "cracking of the roots of trees, the
breaking of boughs, the noise of its hedgewood breaking, the
gaping of the ground, and the riving of the earth asunder; the falling
of the torn furrows" could all be heard. Changes are taking place to

this very day, and some of the meadows have altered their shape and form considerably over the centuries. It is a restless earth, yet to the casual visitor a sense of timeless wonder emanates from a land that bears little mark of modern technology or change when viewed from a hilltop perch. And below there stretches a world of green.

Many miles of footpath and trackway explore the ridge; sometimes overlooking the Weald to the south, sometimes peering northward at the downs. Some explore secretive little valleys. Some take us into the Holmesdale Valley between the greensand and the North Downs. Others tease with a beckoning call down to the very edge of the Weald itself.

Between the Surrey border and Sevenoaks, hill villages and hamlets like Crockham Hill, French Street, Toys Hill, Ide Hill and Weald (Sevenoaks Weald) all offer a variety of outings of great charm. They are in themselves interesting places with outstanding views, and those who know them best consider this to be among the loveliest corners of the whole south.

Knole is the gem at the heart of Sevenoaks. A huge mansion set in a thousand acres of deer park whose once-proud trees were blasted by the '87 storm - one could spend days wandering there with always something new and interesting to see. From it the ridge stretches on towards the east, inviting us to visit one of England's finest medieval moated manor houses. Ightham Mote is held in a gentle cup of hillside with the Weald easing below. Then there's orchard country between Plaxtol and West Peckham and, east of the Medway, a great slope of blossom that stretches from Yalding almost to the neat parkland of Leeds - whose castle is straight out of a dream.

* * *

WALK 9: WESTERHAM - CROCKHAM HILL - WESTERHAM

Distance:	6¹/₂ miles
Maps:	O.S. Pathfinder 1208 'Sevenoaks & Westerham' 1:25,000
	O.S. Landranger 187 'Dorking, Reigate & Crawley' 1:50,000
Start:	Westerham green (GR: 447540)

Access:	Westerham is on A25 about 6 miles west of Sevenoaks. Bus services from Croydon, Bromley and Sevenoaks
Parking:	Public car park 400 yards east of the green, access from A25
Refreshments:	Pubs and cafés in Westerham, pub in Crockham Hill

Westerham is a pleasant, historic little town that nestles amid some of Kent's finest walking country. Surrey woodlands edge the parish boundaries. To the north rise the downs. To the south the greensand hills. Throughout the surrounding hills and valleys spread footpaths of considerable charm. They explore beechwoods and conifer plantations, shallow valleys like that in which the Darent stream unites a string of little lakes, steeply climbing hillsides with huge views from their summits, rolling meadows overlooking countryside that is both peaceful and seemingly remote.

Through this countryside in past ages roamed and rode the two heroes of the town who guard the green: General James Wolfe, the champion of Quebec who was born here, and Sir Winston Churchill who came to live at nearby Chartwell.

This walk begins by the green where Wolfe waves his sword jubilantly aloft, while Churchill sits slumped in bronze, his back to the church. We wander through Squerryes Park beside the Darent stream, then over the wooded brow of Crockham Hill Common to a marvellous view of the Weald - a view that encompasses parts of three counties and some of the loveliest countryside in all the south-east. From Froghole we descend 134 steps through a steep hillside garden, and cross a couple of fields to Crockham Hill village on the unmarked route of the London Countryway. From here it is but a short step into Surrey for a brief trespass out of Kent. Then up again onto the greensand hills along part of the Vanguard Way, crossing the Greensand Way, and down through more woodlands to Squerryes Park and back to Westerham.

It's a fine walk to tackle at any time of year and at any time of the day or evening. But it's only one of many possibilities available in this justifiably popular corner of our county.

* * *

From the green cross the A25 and go up a few steps between buildings and into an alley marked Water Lane. This leads to a

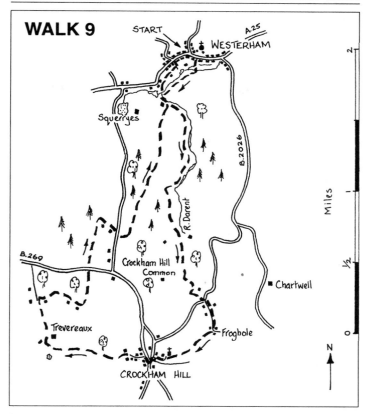

WALK 9

START

WESTERHAM

A.25

Squerryes

B.2026

R. Darent

Miles

B.269

Crockham Hill Common

Chartwell

Trevereaux

Froghole

CROCKHAM HILL

N

branch of the Darent stream and continues to a second branch and into a sloping meadow. Turn right and walk along the lower edge of the meadow, and at its far end cross the Darent again to come onto a track opposite a pond. Turn left and soon come to Park Lodge, passing as you do a few blocks of stone on the left - all that remains of a former water mill. The track swings left in front of Park Lodge and goes through a field gate (GR:444535).

Follow the track through a shallow valley where several little man-made lakes are fed by the young Darent stream. On the left of the lakes mature beech and, later, plantations of pine, hide from view a ruined tower. Immediately before reaching the second lake cross a stile next to a field gate and continue ahead as the track winds through the valley. Eventually it curves to the right away from the lakes and goes through a metal field gate. Do not go through this gate but walk ahead alongside a fence (the track to your left) and come to a stile. Over this bear left and a few yards later cross another stile on the corner of a woodland which disguises the site of an Iron Age hillfort. Over the stile the way now leads along the right-hand edge of a meadow. Two-thirds of the way along this cross yet another stile and go diagonally towards the far left-hand corner where you come to a field gate and another stile. (The Darent rises in the garden of the house to your left.)

Over this stile there is a crossing path. Bear slightly right, then veer left up a narrow, steeply climbing path among trees and rhododendrons on Crockham Hill Common. You are now on the Greensand Ridge. Continue along this path, ignoring alternatives to right and left, and come to a broad crossing path where you turn left. The path curves among trees and comes to another crossing path. Here turn right, and almost immediately go left along a narrow footpath. As you progress along it other trails cut off on either side. Continue ahead until you come to the edge of the common with a clear crossing path where you turn left and wander down a slope with a hedge on your left. (In winter surprise views may be had off to the right overlooking the Weald.) Soon reach the B2026 Westerham-Crockham Hill road (GR: 448514).

Cross the road with great care (it's a blind corner) and walk ahead down Froghole Lane, passing oast houses and a handsome timbered farm. After 300 yards or so the lane makes a sharp left-hand bend by a converted oast house. In the right-hand corner of the lane a signpost directs the path to Crockham Hill church, leading down a flight of stone steps, first beside a tile-hung cottage, Spark Haw (1), then passing a thatched cottage, Buttles Steps Cottage (2), to pass through its garden. As you descend the steps so views open ahead across the Weald of Kent and Surrey, with Sussex shown as the line of Ashdown Forest on the southern horizon.

At the foot of the steps cross a stile and walk down the right-hand side of a field, go over a wooden footbridge and another stile,

Manor Park at West Malling, from where several pleasant walks begin.
(Walk 17)
Orchard country, as seen on the Yalding-Hunton circuit. (Walk 18)

Linton Court, described by Horace Walpole as 'the citadel of Kent, the whole county its garden.' (Walk 19)
Leeds Castle, its foundations planted on an island in a lovely lake. (Walk 20)

then cross an undulating meadow half-left. This was one of the meadows reshaped by the 1596 landslip. The footpath (sometimes rather vague) crosses the meadow, goes through a picnic area, and emerges onto a lane near both Crockham Hill church (3) and the village school. Wander ahead along the lane to its end where you bear left. On coming to a shop cross the main road with care to the village garden, then bear right up the road which forms its boundary. After about 100 yards turn left into Oakdale Lane, passing several cottages, including a converted oast house. Come to a field gate on the left with a stile beside it. Go over the stile and walk down the right-hand edge of a sloping meadow, enjoying more broad vistas of the Weald below, and the curving Greensand Ridge stretching far off to the west until it melts against the horizon.

At the bottom of the field cross a stile and bear right through a woodland. Over a stream and another stile you come into a flat meadow. Cross straight ahead along its right-hand edge and enter a much larger field on the far side. On entering this you leave Kent and come into Surrey. Maintain direction across the field to pass to the left of Trevereaux Manor. On reaching a pond and a solitary oak tree bear half-right to the corner of the field where another stile takes you out opposite a pair of cottages. Turn right and follow a track past the outbuildings of Trevereaux Manor, beyond which you start to rise steadily uphill. This is on the route of the Vanguard Way (4).

The track steepens among trees, and on the right you pass a drive leading to Grace's Cottage (5). Immediately after this a narrow footpath also goes off to the right among trees. Go up this and soon reach a drive. Maintain direction to pass several cottages. Just before it ends (at Scearnbank Bungalow) go through some wooden bars on the left and up a footpath among trees. Come to a crossing track and turn right, soon joining another narrow drive where you again bear right. (Glimpsed views over the Weald.) The drive forks at the entrance to The Scearne; bear left and a few paces later at the entrance to Scearne Bank, take a footpath on the left climbing again among trees. At a junction of paths ignore the right-hand option and continue ahead, still rising uphill, but now on a broader path which leads to a metal gate near a small enclosed reservoir. A few paces later you reach the B269 road near Kent Hatch - the ancient gateway (or 'hatch') between Kent and Surrey (GR:436516).

Cross the road with care and walk directly ahead along a bridleway for a little under half a mile until you come to a water tank. Turn right on a footpath (waymarked Greensand Way) which soon becomes enclosed by fences and leads to a country road at Goodley Stock. Cross to a track leading into more woods. A few yards later come to cross-tracks and turn left. Now walk along this, ignoring alternatives, for about two-thirds of a mile until you emerge from the woods, with the farm buildings of Squerryes Court seen down through a coomb to the left. Continue straight ahead, over a track, through a group of trees and directly ahead over a series of stiles, then down a steep slope of meadow overlooking Westerham (6) and the North Downs beyond. So come to Park Lodge.

Cross the stile beside the lodge and go half-left along the track - which is the same as that used on the outward route. On reaching the pond, instead of branching right on the original path, continue for a few more yards, then take a footpath heading half-right in front of a red tile-hung cottage. This brings you to an attractive cottage-lined lane where you bear left. Reaching the High Street turn right and shortly reach the green once more.

Items of interest:

1: Spark Haw. Originally two cottages with a superb view, and thought to have once been used as an ale house, they were converted to a single dwelling around 1900 by E.V. Lucas, the essayist and publisher. During his time here, Lucas was frequently visited by John Galsworthy and H.G. Wells, and several other notable literary figures of the period.

2: Buttles Steps Cottage garden. A number of springs rise in the garden through which 134 stone steps take the footpath downhill. They form one of the sources of the River Eden, which in turn feeds the Medway. Until piped water was brought to Froghole during the early 20th century, a scoop was provided at one of these springs as the water supply for cottages along the lane. Speculation has it that because of the wildlife attracted to this scoop, the little hamlet gained its name.

3: Crockham Hill church. Dedicated to the Holy Trinity, the church was built in 1842 at the sole expense of Charles Warde of Squerryes Court, Westerham. Beside the altar lies a marble effigy of Octavia Hill, one of the co-founders of the National Trust and a champion of the countryside, who spent some of her happiest days in a house on Crockham Hill Common, and left the express wish that she be buried in the churchyard here. Her grave may be found beneath a large yew tree at the top of the churchyard steps, on the right.

4: The Vanguard Way. Developed in 1980 by the Croydon-based Vanguards Rambling Club, this long-distance walk leads in 62 miles from East Croydon railway station to Seaford Head on the Sussex coast. Guidebooks: *The Vanguard Way* by the Vanguards Rambling Club, and *The Wealdway and The Vanguard Way* by Kev Reynolds (Cicerone Press).

5: Grace's Cottage. On Trevereaux Hill this once belonged to Edward and Constance Garnett who lived nearby in the woods. They were prominent figures in the literary world; she translated Tolstoy and other Russian giants into English, while he was a publisher's reader with enormous influence. During their time there was a constant coming and going of the foremost writers of the day. In Grace's Cottage, rented from the Garnetts, there lived Ford Madox Ford, who played unsuccessfully at farmer as a distraction from his literary career.

6: Westerham. The recent history of Westerham belongs largely to James Wolfe and Winston Churchill. Wolfe was born at The Vicarage in 1727, but spent his boyhood at a multi-gabled house, then known as Spiers, but renamed Quebec House after his famous victory over the French on the Heights of Abraham outside Quebec, at which he won Canada for the British. The house is now in the care of the National Trust and is open to the public. It stands at the eastern end of the town opposite a road which leads to Chartwell, Churchill's home for more than 40 years. This is also open to the public, and is one of the National Trust's most visited properties. At the western end of town is Squerryes Court, a privately owned William and Mary manor house built in 1681, in whose grounds Wolfe received his first commission at the age of only 14. Like Quebec House and Chartwell, this too is open to the public.

WALK 10: DRYHILL (SUNDRIDGE) - MILL BANK WOOD - DRYHILL

Distance:	6 miles
Maps:	O.S. Pathfinder 1208 'Sevenoaks & Westerham' 1:25,000
	O.S. Landranger 188 'Maidstone & The Weald of Kent' 1:50,000
Start:	Dryhill Picnic Park, Sundridge (GR: 498552)
Access:	Signposted south from A25 just west of Sevenoaks By-Pass (A21). Dryhill Lane goes alongside a garden centre on A25.
Parking:	Dryhill Picnic Park (small charge)
Refreshments:	None

This is a farm and woodland walk, with views overlooking the North Downs guarding the Darent Gap, with Polhill looming large on the horizon. Mostly, though, views are restricted, for there are large areas of woodland to be traversed; woods of beech, and oak-lined shaws and conifer plantations, with hazel coppices and here and there holly trees marking the path. Between Mill Bank Wood and Whitley Forest there is a delightful little dale with a spring gushing from a steep bank of greensand, and its stream shortly after feeds a pond that once powered Whitley Mill. Now all that remains of the mill are a few remnants of low walls, moss-covered and with ferns sprouting from the brickwork.

This is a pleasant, undemanding stroll, while Dryhill Picnic Park is a convenient and interesting place in which the less energetic members of the family could happily spend time while the walkers go off exploring.

*   *   *

Leaving the Picnic Park (1) turn left and wander along Dryhill Lane heading south. After Wellers Farm the lane forks. Continue ahead on the approach drive to Dryhill Farm, seeing off to your right the timber-framed house called White Sheiling across a sweep of lawn. Dryhill Farm is also a splendid timbered dwelling, and beyond it the track rises between hedges. Still rising it bears slightly to the right, while to the left there is a gateway.Go through this into the

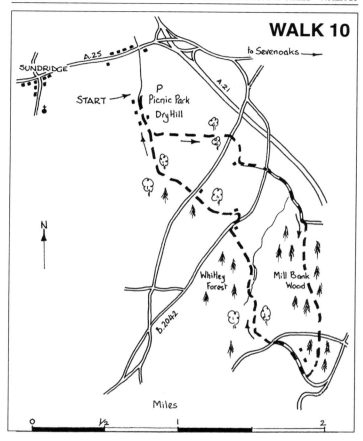

WALK 10

to Sevenoaks →

SUNDRIDGE
A.25
A.21

START →

P
Picnic Park
Dry Hill

N

Whitley
Forest

Mill Bank
Wood

B.2042

Miles

0   ½   1   2

field beyond, and follow the left-hand hedgerow. Ahead, a couple of fields away, is a wood, and as you walk towards it the North Downs are seen off to the left. The footpath continues ahead, and after a while crosses to the left-hand side of the hedgerow to pass along the woodland edge. The path here becomes more of a track and slopes downhill to a narrow road. (Traffic can be seen on the A21 Sevenoaks By-Pass nearby.)

69

Cross to a stile and go up the slope beyond, along the left-hand side of a line of trees. At the top of the field cross another stile and turn right onto a crossing path which leads to farm buildings (Green Lane Farm). Immediately after passing these the track swings left and becomes a narrow lane. In about 400 yards reach the B2042 at a minor crossroads. Go straight over and walk along the lane as it winds downhill. Ignore the footpath sign at the foot of the slope and continue ahead for a total of about half a mile. Eventually a forestry road branches off to the right, and the lane veers leftwards to give a view of a bridge carrying the A21 overhead. Almost immediately after the forestry road turn right at a footpath sign and join a track in a conifer plantation - Mill Bank Wood (GR: 514537) - which is followed for almost a mile. When it forks about halfway along, continue ahead. The track is now surfaced.

Eventually come to a country road with a field gate and a stile opposite. Over the stile wander ahead. (On the left, just beside the gate, will be seen a circular water tank.) Follow the main track through the woods, ignoring side turnings. It makes a slow curve to the right, then slants leftwards, becoming more narrow and leading to another narrow country road. Turn right and walk along the road among trees, and with a couple of isolated houses off to the right, for about 500 yards to a T junction. Turn left and about 30 yards later, cross a stile on the right and go up a slope ahead into Whitley Forest. At the top of the rise the track swings to the right and begins to descend the slope. Halfway down it veers left, and soon after makes a second bend to the left. At this point leave the track and take a minor path to the right.

It leads through trees and crosses a stile. Continue towards an open field. The way now goes between fields along a line of mature trees, and with the dark conifers of Whitley Forest making almost a complete circle round this large space of farmland. When the path forks beneath a line of telegraph wires continue ahead and descend into a pleasant little valley where you bear right to wander through it. A few yards along this a stream emerges from a spring gushing from under a greensand bank on the right. Keeping ahead the path now goes through a field gate and begins to wind round the hillside. Soon the reedy pond that once turned Whitley Mill is seen to the right; at its end low walls are all that remain.

Keep to the main path/track that winds away to the left, now climbing a steady incline and following to the left of a line of telegraph poles up towards the forest edge, and with a large rolling field to the right. The track eventually brings you to a road once more (GR: 505536). To the right stands Whitley Farm, with farm buildings opposite. Turn right and walk along the B2042 for 100 yards or so. Where it curves to the right break away half-left towards a cottage. (The hedges in front of the cottage are trimmed into imaginative topiary figures.) Turn left in front of the cottage and follow a track that soon becomes a footpath at the end of the cottage garden.

The path is enclosed by trees and holly bushes, drops downhill and enters Green Lane Wood. Come to a country lane next to Beech Tree Cottage and turn left for a few paces, then to the right over a stile giving access into the bottom corner of a field. Walk up the slope with a hazel coppice woodland to your left, and at the top corner of the field veer left to cross a track, then bear right. So enter the corner of another field. Walk along its right-hand headland, with long views ahead to the North Downs, and with a woodland to your right. On reaching the far right-hand corner go through a gateway onto an enclosed track which leads all the way back to Dryhill Picnic Park.

Items of interest:

1: Dryhill Picnic Park. Some 22 acres of spinney and open space, with mounds and hollows betraying the fact that it was once a quarry for Kentish ragstone. The steep outcrops are honeycombed with rabbit warrens. There is a picnic area with tables and benches; public toilets and a tap providing drinking water; and a small car parking area. The Park closes at dusk.

WALK 11: SEVENOAKS WEALD - BORE PLACE - SEVENOAKS WEALD

Distance:	7 miles
Maps:	O.S. Pathfinder 1208 'Sevenoaks & Westerham' and 1228 'Tonbridge & Edenbridge' 1:25,000

	O.S. Landranger 188 'Maidstone & The Weald of Kent' 1:50,000
Start:	Weald church (GR: 528514)
Access:	By minor road heading west from A21 and A225 south of Sevenoaks
Parking:	In a lay-by north of the church at junction of Church Road and Glebe Road
Refreshments:	Pubs and shop in Weald

Without laying claim to be overly pretty, Sevenoaks Weald is a charming place whose greatest asset is the great plunging vista that spreads away from its doors. Surrounded by hills and moulded valleys, cottages, timbered houses and attractive farms are scattered about the meadows, while the village itself has a number of dwellings lining the streets with an air of belonging, rooted several generations old. In the past Weald attracted one or two poets, for that restless individual Edward Thomas once lived here, and 'Supertramp' W.H. Davies wrote his classic autobiography in a cottage found for him by Thomas. It was here too, that Harold Nicolson and Vita Sackville-West set up home at Long Barn on the edge of the village before moving on to Sissinghurst.

Our walk begins and ends in the village, but the circuit explores an undulating landscape where there are no centres of habitation, no villages or hamlets, just an odd collection of farms and cottages snug below the greensand hills. And a constant delight of unfolding panoramas. It visits the fringe of a bird reserve at Winkhurst Green, and wanders through the grounds of historic Bore Place where a long-running project of environmental agriculture is in progress. The Commonwork Centre here runs a variety of courses, and is an exciting place to visit on its occasional Open Days.

*   *   *

Just north of the church of St George, Church Road and Glebe Road form a junction. A few yards uphill from this cross a stile on the left next to a metal gate, and walk along the left-hand edge of a field on the route of the Greensand Way. The Greensand Ridge stretches into the distance ahead. Come to some gorse bushes, go over another stile, descend the slope and cross a small brook, then climb towards Dale Farm seen at the head of the slope. There you cross

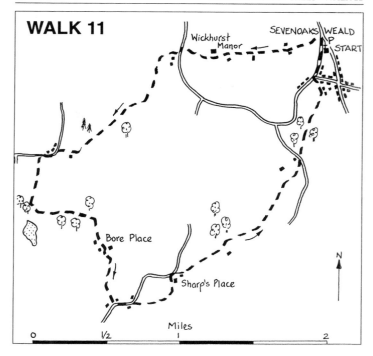

WALK 11

Wickhurst Manor

SEVENOAKS WEALD

P START

Bore Place

Sharp's Place

N

Miles

0   ½   1   2

another stile and bear right along the farm drive. Passing a converted oast house the way swings right, then left between farm buildings to enter a field. Wander across to a screen of trees on the far side, then over the next field to more trees, beyond which will be seen a large collection of farm buildings. Heading a little to the left go down to a ditch, then pass to the right of the buildings (GR: 521512).

The way leads into another field where you aim half-left towards another line of trees to gain a first view of Wickhurst Manor (1) ahead. Descend to a stile giving onto a driveway opposite the Manor's entrance gates. Bear left, then turn right where the drive forks a few paces later. This leads past the Manor and on to a large dutch barn. Pass along the left-hand side of the barn and crossing a stile enter a long sloping meadow. Go up this to the top right-hand

73

corner, and over a stile come onto a country lane. Bear left towards Hatchlands Farm.

Just before reaching the farm turn sharp right to cross a stile and walk along the left-hand edge of a field, then by way of other stiles into a larger field behind the farm itself. There are two paths. Ignore that which goes off to the right (the Greensand Way), and instead cut across the field ahead, passing farm buildings and making for the far left-hand corner. On the way you pass below a series of slurry pits. In the field corner go over a plank footbridge linking two stiles, then walk along the left headland of a very large field, alongside a drainage ditch.

Walk the complete length of this field, and in the far corner you will find two more stiles. Cross the right-hand stile into the field ahead on the right, then go left immediately to follow the field edge and maintain your general direction. Following the hedgerow you reach yet another stile. Cross over and follow the left-hand fence dividing two fields and come to a line of trees. Through these cross an open field with lovely views to the greensand hills, and head towards the left-hand corner of the wood seen ahead. Follow the woodland boundary, still in the same direction, and come to a field stretching to the right of a house. Walk across the field, keeping parallel with the left-hand fence, and drop down the slope to find another stile in the bottom left-hand corner. This brings you onto a lane opposite a pair of cottages (GR: 500501).

Turn left and follow the lane as it bends to the right past Scollops Farm. Just before it crosses a small brook, leave the lane and enter the field on the left. Walk along its right-hand boundary. This leads to the edge of a woodland with a footbridge and another path heading to the right. Ignore these and continue round the field, seeing as you do the lagoon created by Bough Beech Reservoir (2) a short distance away. Remain along the headland of the field and soon come to a second, much larger, woodland. Keep this to your right until you reach a gateway by an oak tree. Go through the gateway and bear right on a track that leads all the way to Bore Place (3).

Wander through the farmyard, passing the Tudor manor house off to your left. The concrete farm road bears left and joins the main driveway which you follow to its end. Here join a country lane by a small barn and with an old brick-built house to the right with the date 1745 scratched in the mortar above the front door. Turn left along the lane and about 100 yards later note the old water pump on the left, standing among hedges (4).

The lane makes a sharp left-hand bend by some cottages. Straight ahead, and beside a telegraph pole, a marker stone directs the continuing path up among some trees to a stile and into a field. Bear half-left over this to find the next stile a little to the left of a woodland corner. Continue uphill along the edge of the little woodland shaw, and follow round the headland to find another stile set behind another telegraph pole. Over this go diagonally half-left across the field towards yet another telegraph pole, with fine views again to the greensand hills. In the field corner behind it, by an oak tree, cross into the next field and walk ahead towards the left-hand edge of a hedgerow beyond which you will see a farmhouse. This is Sharp's Place (GR: 513487). Continue in the same direction down the slope to come onto a country road at a sharp corner.

Walk ahead along the road for a few yards, then bear right on a farm track which you follow uphill. It sweeps to the left between barns and enters a field. Go diagonally across this to the far left-hand corner where you cross a footbridge, go over a stile and bear left. In a few yards turn right along an enclosed track going towards Hale Oak Farm. About 80 yards along it cross a stile on the left and then go over the field towards a woodland. Enter the next field by the woodland corner and walk ahead with the wood on your left. There are fine views to the right, and at the bottom of the slope stands Hale Oak Farm.

Keep alongside the wood through two fields, but when it ends cross two stiles into the field on the left. Wander across the field and pass to the left of a crown of trees. Halfway down the next slope cross two more stiles, and at the foot of the slope go over a footbridge above a deeply cut brook. Continue straight ahead to another stile and a footbridge spanning a more substantial brook than before. Over a short steep slope now, with farm buildings ahead and to the left, then follow to the right of a hedge about 100 yards or so away from the dutch barn and other farm buildings seen off to your left. In the far corner of the field another stile leads onto a lane just to the right of a cottage (GR: 526501).

Cross the lane and walk ahead along a bridleway among trees. There is also a footpath sign to the left. Both routes lead back to Sevenoaks Weald, and in the event of the bridleway being badly cut and muddy, it may be preferable to use the footpath. Otherwise walk straight ahead along the track, noting the lovely old house called Long Barn (5) off to the left. The track gradually rises to a beech hedge with houses behind it, then forks. Go left and soon reach the village green. Bear right across the green and come to Church Road, directly opposite The Windmill pub. Follow Church Road back to the church.

Items of interest:

1: Wickhurst Manor. Although most of this manor house dates from the 19th century, it contains a large medieval hall and a stone doorway from the 15th. An elegant, imposing house.

2: Bough Beech Reservoir. Created by the East Surrey Water Company in the late 1960s by damming and flooding a valley south of Winkhurst Green. The northern part of the reservoir is a wildfowl reserve that has become an important breeding site. Viewing is from

a narrow public road between the main reservoir and the lagoons to the north. On the edge of the reservoir at Winkhurst Green an oast house has been converted as an information centre manned by volunteers from the Kent Trust for Nature Conservation. Upstairs, in the oast roundel, is a small but interesting museum to the hop industry. (See also Walk 21.)

This old pump is found in a hedgerow near Bore Place

3: Bore Place. A fascinating Tudor manor on whose farm an environmental project was set up by the late Neil Wates. The Commonwork Centre based on the farm runs courses (residential and non-residential) on ecology and history. There is a field trail and leaflets are available when open.

4: Hand pump. This old water pump, half-hidden by hedges and a tangle of brambles, was used until the 1960s as the sole water supply for nearby cottages.

5: Long Barn. This lovely old timbered house is said to have been the birthplace of William Caxton. Long Barn dates from the 14th century, but was restored in 1915 after having been used as labourers' cottages. Harold Nicolson and Vita Sackville-West laid out the gardens during their period in residence here, before moving on to Sissinghurst Castle. After the Nicolsons, Long Barn was bought in 1936 by American aviator Charles Lindbergh, who made the first solo transatlantic flight in May 1927.

WALK 12: SEVENOAKS (KNOLE) - IGHTHAM MOTE - KNOLE

Distance:	7 miles
Maps:	O.S. Pathfinder 1208 'Sevenoaks & Westerham' 1:25,000
	O.S. Landranger 188 'Maidstone & The Weald of Kent' 1:50,000
Start:	Knole Park, Sevenoaks (GR: 535543)
Access:	Knole Park has several entrances. The one to use is that which is opposite the church of St Nicholas at the southern end of Sevenoaks High Street. Nearest railway station: Sevenoaks
Parking:	Several approved car parks in the town. (*Not* in Knole Park.)
Refreshments:	Pubs, cafés and shops in Sevenoaks

Set in its thousand-acre deer park, Knole is one of England's largest historic houses. It has 365 rooms and a staircase for every week of the year. Not far away, and nestling in a bowl of wooded hills, sits Ightham Mote, an idyllic moated manor house dating from the 14th century - arguably the finest in all Britain.

Between them the Greensand Ridge is topped by beech, oak and chestnut, but open here and there after natural thinning by storm to provide stunning views over the great expanse of the Weald. Along the ridge there are many viewpoints and footpaths, some of which have been linked as part of the Greensand Way. But there are other paths too that are also worth exploring. Paths that delve into hidden patches of countryside 'inland' - away from the crest - without the views, but not without charm.

This walk has much to commend it. You could begin by photographing the herds of fallow deer that graze Knole Park, then spend an hour or so visiting the house (open to the public by the National Trust) before heading along the spine of the hills. Upon arrival at Ightham Mote there are temptations to linger too, for at certain times this also is open to the public by the National Trust. The return to Knole branches away from the outward route heading slightly 'inland', but not before gaining a glorious viewpoint. All in all a splendid outing.

*   *   *

Opposite the 12th-century church of St Nicholas in Sevenoaks High Street, walk down the drive to the entrance gates to Knole Park, pass the lodge and enter the neat rolling parkland with its grazing deer. Follow the drive down the initial slope,

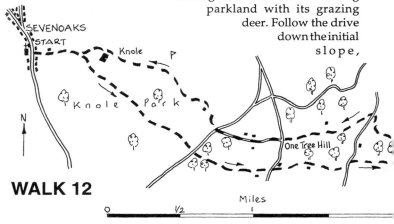

WALK 12

and at the bottom take a metalled footpath waymarked as a link path for the Greensand Way. About 100 yards later take another fork right with the huge frontage of Knole House (1) before you. Bear half-right on a vague grass path (Greensand Way) to pass alongside the right-hand boundary wall of Knole House. At the far end continue straight ahead still on the Greensand Way link path. The way veers left, crosses a narrow driveway and goes ahead on another drive for several hundred yards. At a T junction of metalled tracks (formerly known as Chestnut Walk) go straight ahead on another grass path which is used by the official Greensand Way. Shortly after this leave Knole Park through a gate in a high deer fence (GR: 549531).

Cross the road and continue ahead on a narrow path through mixed woods, and soon reach a stile leading into a field used as a riding paddock. Turn right and walk round the field boundary, making for the far right-hand corner where you will find another stile. Go over this and 15 yards later bear left on an enclosed footpath with big views to the right and a hazel coppice on the left.

The footpath leads behind a house and shortly after brings you onto its drive, then a quiet lane. Leave the Greensand Way here (we rejoin it later) and cross the lane to continue along a track below a house. Views are once more compelling. Along the track the way forks. Take the left-hand option, and after passing White Rocks Farm go straight ahead on a path, initially following a fence. When you come to another very narrow lane turn left along it for about 15 yards, then bear right on the continuing footpath, once more rejoining the Greensand Way. It leads among trees, enters National Trust land and eventually brings you to isolated Wilmot Cottage (2) (GR:574529).

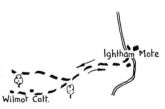

Continue ahead on a track with a little vignette of a view showing the distant church of Shipbourne down in the open Weald. The way leads past a little woodland that is a riot of bluebells and wild garlic in spring, and eventually brings you to a farmyard with some oast houses. (Note the wooden owl perched in one of the oast cowls.) Bear left and come to a country road. Turn right and a few yards later, on the left, is the entrance to Ightham Mote (3) (GR: 585535).

The return to Knole Park retraces the last third of a mile of the outward route. Leaving the oast houses of the farm behind, wander up the track until you come to a stile set beside a gate. Just before this veer right on another track climbing alongside fields. Near the crown of the hill an extensive panorama is worth studying. This is Wilmot Hill. Pause for a moment to capture the views, then slope down to enter woods, where the path tends to be muddy at times, and continue ahead, rising uphill again. On coming to a T junction of paths bear right and soon come to a lane. Cross this onto a path which continues among woods. It rises and falls, has various branches to it, and is muddy in places where horses have cut the soft ground.

Eventually come to an open field on the right, with a strangely narrow white house standing in it. A National Trust sign for One Tree Hill is on the left. (More large views may be had by making a short diversion onto it.) Continue straight ahead at cross-tracks for Knole Park, still rising in the woods. Remain ahead (there is a narrow bridleway which is often muddy, with a footpath on its left) and soon come to a road junction. Cross over and take that which is straight ahead and signposted to River Hill and Sevenoaks. Walk along it for about $1/2$ mile until you reach another road junction (GR: 552534). Knole Park lies ahead.

Enter the Park. Along the broad metalled track bear right at a junction and walk ahead past Keeper's Cottage and over the golf course. The track leads in front of Knole House where you then rejoin the path leading back into Sevenoaks.

Items of interest:

1: Knole House. Begun in 1456 by Archbishop of Canterbury, Thomas Bourchier, Knole grew on an extravagant scale; built of local ragstone round three main courtyards - grey brooding walls and towers and countless windows. Henry VIII took it over in 1532. Elizabeth I gave it to Sir Thomas Sackville, first Earl of Dorset, who set about remodelling and extending it. It has been with the Sackvilles ever since. Now in the care of the National Trust, Knole's doors are open to the public. Inside its treasures include rare antiques and

Knole Park in Sevenoaks has its own large herd of fallow deer

tapestries, and an art collection containing works by Gainsborough and Reynolds, among others. And outside, of course, the magnificent parkland with its many deer roaming with little regard for human visitors.

2: Wilmot Cottage. This isolated cottage, enjoying fine views, is thought to have once been an ale house when the track past its doors was a pack-horse route.

3: Ightham Mote. Presented to the National Trust in 1985, Ightham Mote is a magnificent place, the perfect medieval moated manor house; mellow stone, ancient timbers, lived in since 1340. It has a Great Hall that is a real gem. From it a 14th-century doorway leads to an early 17th-century staircase. There is a Tudor chapel and a crypt with walls 4 feet thick. There are two stone bridges across the moat; lichen crusted, moss-soft, the water of the moat fed by springs, and in it ducks and geese and swans. The house, its setting, its history, all combine to make Ightham Mote one of the truly remarkable sites of Kent.

WALK 13: IGHTHAM - OLDBURY HILL - RASPIT HILL - IGHTHAM

Distance:	5 miles
Maps:	O.S. Pathfinder 1208 'Sevenoaks & Westerham' 1:25,000
	O.S. Landranger 188 'Maidstone & The Weald of Kent' 1:50,000
Start:	Ightham Village Hall (GR: 594566)
Access:	Turn off A25 opposite The Cob Tree Inn. The village hall is found a short distance along this road on the left
Parking:	Behind the village hall
Refreshments:	Pubs in Ightham and at Crown Point

This is a walk into history. Beginning in Ightham village with some fine old buildings, it soon leads to the high woodlands of Oldbury Hill where, in about 100 B.C., Iron Age man created a hillfort. There have been a great number of important discoveries made here, the majority of which were the result of a lifetime's passion by Benjamin Harrison, the Ightham grocer, who collected tens of thousands of flints, including Neolithic tools much older than archaeologists had previously realised were used.

Almost the entire length of the walk is through woodlands, so distant views will be more hinted at than seen. But it's an interesting walk for all that, and not simply from the crossing of Oldbury Hill's ancient site. The woodlands are lovely in themselves - and remarkably little affected by the '87 storm - with a good mixture of oak and beech and sweet chestnut and birch giving a blend of colour and texture. Near Raspit Hill there comes a feeling of space with the Weald hinted beyond the tree-screen, and the discovery of a string of pools within the woods makes a tempting site for a picnic.

*   *   *

On leaving the car park behind the village hall, turn right and walk through Ightham to reach the busy A25. A pedestrian footbridge allows a safe crossing to be made. Go to The Cob Tree Inn and turn along Oldbury Lane which runs beside it. This leads for about a

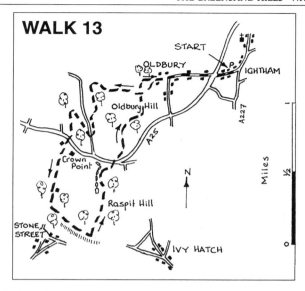

WALK 13

START

OLDBURY

IGHTHAM

Oldbury Hill

A227

A25

Crown
Point

Miles

N

Raspit Hill

STONE
STREET

IVY HATCH

third of a mile, passing a number of houses and a primary school, and shortly after this, Old Bury Hall, a fine 15th-century timbered hall house on your left. The lane leads directly to The Coach House. Follow a bridleway alongside the house. It begins to rise, soon becoming a deeply sunken track that makes a passage through a veritable cleft, with trees overhanging. At the top of the slope come to a junction of several paths near the north-eastern corner of Oldbury Hill (1) (GR: 584564).

Continue straight ahead along a path with orchards a short distance away to the right, and follow this for almost a third of a mile, until you come to a major path junction. There are paths to right and left, and three that go ahead, almost parallel with each other. Take the left-hand of these three paths. After about 50 yards it swings sharply to the left at the edge of a steep slope where you can see the rooftops of several houses below at Styants Bottom. Deep in the leaf-mould of centuries the footpath follows round near the edge of the slope, still among trees. Through them to the right you can see to the hills lining the narrow valley on the western side.

Eventually you come to a marker post in the middle of the path, with a flight of timber-braced steps leading down the slope. Go down the steps, and on reaching the foot of the slope continue ahead towards a narrow country lane. A few paces before it, come to a cross-track and bear left for a few hundred yards until it brings you to the lane itself opposite a parking and picnic area. Cross the lane, but immediately before reaching an overhead barrier at its entrance, turn half-right along a bridleway. About 150 yards later join a broad path slanting leftwards. In effect this means almost doubling back. The path rises a little on the approach to the A25, which is met opposite a stone-built cottage, with the Crown Point Inn below in a hollow.

Cross the road with care towards the cottage (GR: 575558). Now wander ahead along a driveway that runs down the side of the cottage, and follow to its end beside a house. An enclosed bridleway continues beyond the house and rises among woods. At the head of the slope you reach a field gate, with a cross-track beyond. Turn left, still among trees, and soon with a steeply plunging slope to your right, mostly hidden by trees, although you can sense the great open spaces of the Weald beyond. (Much of this slope was at one time quarried.)

Continue along the track, which follows the rim of the slope above Stone Street, until the woods on the left fall away into a hollow, with the track going ahead along a narrow crest. There are lovely views from this crest; expansive views worth pausing to contemplate. Bear left on an alternative path that descends into a pleasant little wooded valley, and follow through to meet a string of six small ponds which form an attractive picture and make a convenient site for a picnic.

On reaching the fourth pool the path forks. Take the right fork which leads to the A25 again. Cross over to find a bus-stop pull-in a little way to the right where the road becomes dual carriageway. Behind it, on the edge of woods, there's a junction of bridleways. Take that which climbs to the right, sloping above the road on an embankment. It swings left and begins to cut a way through the hillside bank, but a little short of this turn right on a crossing track and climb a few steps. A broad track now takes you along the eastern edge of Oldbury Hill, in trees all the way. Shortly after it curves leftwards you come to a junction of paths and go straight ahead. A few yards later reach more converging paths - at the top of the cleft through which the outward track led. Instead of turning right here, continue ahead to the woodland edge, then bear right on another path which soon becomes a sunken track descending the wooded slopes. Come to Oldbury Lane once more near The Coach House and wander back to Ightham.

Items of interest:

1: Oldbury Hill. An Iron Age hillfort dating from about 100 B.C., it covers 151 acres and is thought to have originated from Wealden tribes. It was later taken over by Belgic settlers who barricaded it against the Romans, and it has been speculated that the position of the site indicates a portion of one of the rare north-south trackways through the Weald which was then, of course, a thick and extensive forest. There are rock shelters on the eastern side of Oldbury Hill that were apparently used by Palaeolithic hunters. Not far from these a spring oozes to this day, where for all the days of Oldbury's occupation water would have been drawn for the use of all those encamped there.

WALK 14: SHIPBOURNE - IGHTHAM MOTE - SHIPBOURNE

Distance:	4 miles
Maps:	O.S. Pathfinder 1208 'Sevenoaks & Westerham' 1:25,000
	O.S. Landranger 188 'Maidstone & The Weald of Kent' 1:50,000
Start:	Shipbourne church (GR: 594523)
Access:	Shipbourne is on A227 (Tonbridge-Gravesend) road, about 3½ miles north of Tonbridge
Parking:	In a lay-by on Upper Green Road opposite the church
Refreshments:	Pub in Shipbourne

Shipbourne is an uncrowded, spacious village in the midst of a walker's countryside. To the north rise the greensand hills, but around the village there are long vistas of field, meadow and woodland. Little brooks and streams curl though gentle valleys. Footpaths lead everywhere, and take the rambler to many memorable places: to Ightham Mote, to Old Soar Manor, Plaxtol and Mereworth Woods, through Fairlawne Park and along the Greensand Ridge.

This outing is short, easy and quite lovely. It explores the slopes of greensand, wanders through meadows and over fields, into woods where birds sing bright and early, and foxes and rabbits scuttle in the undergrowth. And it visits splendid Ightham Mote. Along the hills our path follows a stretch of the Greensand Way, and as it does, so huge views are opened onto the green acres of the Weald.

*   *   *

Enter the churchyard of St Giles by the lych gate, and walk round the right-hand side of the church to a wooden gate in the western wall giving access to a large field. Three paths branch away, but they are not always evident on the ground. Bear right and walk along the edge of the field to pass the boundary of a large house with an oast beside it. Come to a stile in the corner and cross it. Go ahead over a second stile and on a continuing footpath to a double field gate on the far side of the field, where there is yet another stile. Ignore the Greensand Way which goes directly ahead, and bear half-right along a track.

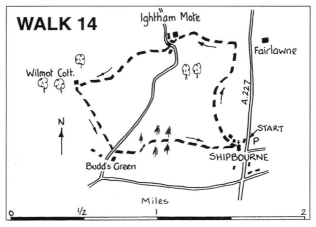

The moat at Ightham Mote

Separated from a sports ground by a hedge, the way passes a pavilion. Cross a stony track and continue ahead up a slope with a hedgerow on the left. Cross a stile beside a field gate and pause for a moment to study the views back to the south and east. It's a rolling country of broad panoramas with fine trees spaced here and there; attractive at all times of the year.

Continue in the same direction. Ahead, half-right, stands the great mansion of Fairlawne (see Walk 15). On reaching more farm gates go through a single gate beside them, and about 100 yards later find a stile beside a gate on the left, which gives access to an enclosed bridleway (being used by horses it can be muddy). Walking down the bridleway oast houses are seen ahead to the right, with the greensand hills behind them. To the left meadows fold away towards woods and the open spaces of the Weald.

The track leads out of its avenue of hedges, and winds downhill. Suddenly you find yourself beside the moat and wonderful timber-and-stone frontage of Ightham Mote (1) (GR: 585535). It's a marvellous sight, breathing history and elegance in its mellow walls, and tranquillity with the ducks paddling to and fro in the lilied waters of the moat.

Continue on the drive past the old manor house and out to a country lane. Here turn right for a few yards, then left towards a farmyard with oast houses completing a charming picture (see Walk 12). Just before the oasts a farm track heads off to the right, going uphill between fields. Wander along it, and when it forks soon after, continue on the main track (the right-hand option), but before doing so take the opportunity to enjoy views back the way you have just come.

The track divides again. Ahead (the left-hand track) a metal field gate takes you beside a broadening woodland shaw in which masses of bluebells and wild garlic flower in springtime. The way continues and as the trees thin out so another glorious panorama may be enjoyed across the Weald; an expanse of meadow and woodland and distant hill, with Shipbourne church seen far off, and the distant horizon a veil of blue undulating with its hint of more fine country waiting to be explored.

On the right stands Wilmot Cottage (2), gazing into the view. On the left a stile is signposted to Little Butts. Cross this and go down the meadowland straight ahead to a second stile. Over this views are perhaps even better than at Wilmot Cottage, for you now see the curving line of the greensand hills as a backdrop to the spacious Weald. Walk ahead along the right-hand side of the field, over another stile, maintaining direction, so to find a plank footbridge. Over the next field come to a country lane and turn right for a few yards (GR: 577523).

Immediately before reaching the entrance to a house turn left, over a stile and along a grassy pathway rising up a slope. At the top of the rise the track forks. Go left and walk downhill beside chestnut trees and larches. Come to a junction of paths and take the second path on the right, which will be seen to run along the edge of the plantation with fields beyond. This brings you to a stile in the corner of the plantation, and an open view across a field to Shipbourne church (3). A footpath leads directly to it.

Items of interest:

1: Ightham Mote. Often described as Britain's finest example of a medieval moated manor house, it dates back to 1340 and is now in the care of the National Trust. (See expanded notes that accompany

Walk 12.)

2: Wilmot Cottage. Enjoying solitude and a wonderful view, this cottage is thought to have once been an ale house in the days when the trackway past its door was a busy pack-horse route.

3: Shipbourne. A small, straggling village consisting of a handful of houses, The Chaser pub and a Victorian reconstruction (Early English in style) for its church. Gargoyles stare down from the tower, and there's a coffin-rest at the lych gate. Nearby, partly in Plaxtol, stands the great house of Fairlawne (see Walk 15).

WALK 15: SHIPBOURNE - OLD SOAR - PLAXTOL - SHIPBOURNE

Distance:	5 miles
Maps:	O.S. Pathfinder 1208 'Sevenoaks & Westerham' and 1209 'Maidstone' 1:25,000
	O.S. Landranger 188 'Maidstone & The Weald of Kent' 1:50,000
Start:	Shipbourne green (GR: 594523)
Access:	Shipbourne is on A227 (Tonbridge-Gravesend) road, about 3½ miles north of Tonbridge
Parking:	In a lay-by on Upper Green Road opposite the church
Refreshments:	Pubs in Shipbourne, Dunks Green and Plaxtol

There are several notable features of this walk, any one of which would be excuse enough to tackle it. Link them together and you have a superb outing. There are orchards, heady with blossom in springtime, views of distant hills and gentle valleys. There are streams that twist through meadows, delightful pools and waterfalls in Fairlawne Park, the great spreading acres of parkland - a scene of peace and beauty. There's the hillside village of Plaxtol, with its attractive houses, its handsome church with typical Kentish weatherboarded cottages lining the road beside it. And there's Old Soar Manor, a 13th-century ragstone building cared for by the National Trust.

*　　　*　　　*

Walk along Upper Green Road away from the church. The road curves to the right, but on the left, by the side of 1 New Cottages, a footpath cuts away beside a wall and alongside a garage, crosses a stile and enters a field. Wander down the field on the path of the Greensand Way (1); cross a stream at the bottom and continue up the far side towards the grey stone buildings of Fairlawne Home Farm. A farm access road now takes you ahead to a country lane. Cross to a gate with a stile beside it and walk across the field beyond, slightly left of the crown of the field (should the footpath be unclear on the ground) making for a vague gap in the line of trees ahead. As you approach you will see a stile leading into the woods.

Take the left-hand of two paths down through the corner of woodland to a field on the far side. Here a path is seen going straight across the field (the Greensand Way), but our route bears half-right to the far corner where a stile is set against a large block of stone. To the right is a plantation (a *platt*) of nut trees. Cross the stile and walk along the edge of a small field to a country road at Dunks Green (GR: 612526). Turn left and soon come to a road junction by The Kentish Rifleman pub.

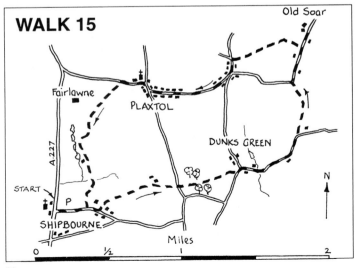

Take the lane to the right leading in front of the pub, sloping gently down to cross the River Bourne (2). Beyond this the lane passes the few houses of Roughway, and is then banked by orchards on either side. The lane bends to the right, with Roughway Farm on the left; an impressive farm in a commanding position. Immediately before it a footpath breaks away to the left to enter an orchard. With farm buildings on the right the track now leads into another orchard with big views of the greensand hills, and Plaxtol adorning the hillside across the valley. At the head of the slope walk alongside a field of soft fruit, then more orchards with a continuing splendid vista of distant orchards, meadows and far-off hills. So much fine country put to good use; husbandry mingled with the art of nature.

On reaching the end of the orchards go through a gate next to a metal field gate. Bear left on an enclosed path as far as a narrow country lane. Here turn right along Old Soar Road. Passing Broadfield Farm there are orchards everywhere, and white-tipped oast houses adding distinctive features. The lane sweeps down to cross one of many tributaries of the Bourne stream, then climbs past cottages and a little further on reaches Old Soar Manor standing on the left-hand side of the lane (3) (GR: 619542). If it is open it would be worth spending a few minutes looking round it.

Having looked at Old Soar, retrace your footsteps back down to the little stream, and then leave the lane by way of a stile beside a field gate on the right. Walk down a track next to an orchard, with the stream to your left. When the track curves to the right, leave it and follow a vague path along the right bank of the stream as it winds through a shallow valley. On reaching a fence cross by another stile, go over a ditch and follow the left-hand edge of the field beyond. Passing beneath power cables you come to a sturdy wooden footbridge crossing the lovely River Bourne, here a clear winding stream with an urgency to its flow. On the far side walk up a small field to reach a lane. Turn left into Plaxtol Spout.

Bear right on reaching a junction, to pass in front of a 15th-century timber-framed building used as a showroom for an art metal work factory, and walk uphill into Plaxtol proper. It's a pleasant hillside village with a number of good buildings, and with pubs and one or two shops. Bear right at the end of the main street towards the church, seen overlooking the village. In front stands a war memorial. Behind is a row of typical Kentish weatherboarded cottages to complete a pretty scene. Bear left in front of the church, passing the cottages on your right. Still along the road there is an estate wall on the left. Beyond it there are surprising views south into the Weald. About 200 yards from the church come to a break in the wall, with a field gate and a stile beside it. Cross the stile and enter Fairlawne Park (4).

A glorious landscape opens before you. Parkland rolls away, green and lush, with stands of mature trees serving almost as islands in this sea of green. The country slopes off to the south, turning from green to watery blue as distance swallows individual features and washes all the world with its soft and delicious light. Gazing eastwards we see the Greensand Ridge folding with lumpy projections off to the cut of the Medway near Yalding, unseen but vaguely hinted several miles away. Then to the right, stately trees obscure much of Fairlawne's grave red-brick façade, but this will soon be partially displayed as our route wanders in front of it.

There is no footpath to be seen, but the way goes half-right from the stile, towards that panorama of space. Find a second stile in a fence about 100 yards from the inner wall of the estate. An unusual memorial wall is seen to the left. Over another stile maintain direction (marker poles aid route finding) to reach a fence and stile below the estate wall. Cross the stile and continue in the same direction, now with a clear view of the front of the Fairlawne mansion over your right shoulder.

Parkland leads you on, still without a path to be seen. Come to another fence with a stile immediately to the left of a bank of laurel bushes. Over this the greensward drops to a narrow estate drive, and beyond it a series of pools feeding one into another, flowing down from the house. The whole area has been landscaped in a most charming manner, and one feels privileged to have this opportunity to wander through such an exquisite scene.

Bear left along the drive for a short distance, and where it forks take the right-hand drive leading directly in front of some buildings below the largest of the pools. Keeping the buildings on your right go ahead to reach a wooden field gate with a small pedestrian gate beside it. Follow the path beyond, over a concrete footbridge, now with views to the right along the Greensand Ridge, and up the sloping field ahead. At the top the path leads between garden hedges and out to a road which crosses Shipbourne village green. Turn right here, so to arrive back near the church.

Items of interest:

1: The Greensand Way. A superb long-distance route which links Haslemere in Surrey with Hamstreet near Ashford in Kent. 110 miles of scenic walking. KCC has published a colourful route guide to the Kent half of the walk: *Greensand Way in Kent* by Bea Cowan. Waymarking for the Kent section is first class.

2: River Bourne. A small stream, perhaps, but one whose power has been harnessed in the past to power mills for the papermaking industry. Where the lane crosses on our route, you can see Roughway Mill to the left.

3: Old Soar Manor. A ragstone manor house dating from 1290; the solar, chapel and undercrofts that remain are open to the public. The Queen Anne farmhouse to which it is attached, and which replaces the original hall, is private.

4: Fairlawne. A large and somewhat curious mansion of brick and ragstone, it overlooks extensive parkland and the Weald beyond. Here was born that critic of Cromwell, Sir Harry Vane. But it is likely that the rambler will better remember the rhododendrons, the pools and cascades, rather than the house or the man who lived there and was beheaded in June 1662, although it is said that he walks through the grounds with his head beneath his arm, accompanied by his wife, on the anniversary of his death.

WALK 16: HADLOW - WEST PECKHAM - HADLOW

Distance:	8 miles
Maps:	O.S. Pathfinder 1209 'Maidstone' and 1229 'Paddock Wood & Staplehurst' 1:25,000
	O.S. Landranger 188 'Maidstone & The Weald of Kent' 1:50,000
Start:	Hadlow (GR: 634497)

Access:	Hadlow is about 3½ miles north-east of Tonbridge on A26 (Tonbridge-Maidstone) road
Parking:	With discretion in the High Street
Refreshments:	Pubs in Hadlow and West Peckham

Hadlow is noted for the Gothic tower that rises 170 feet above its broad street, dominating the countryside for miles around. 'May's Folly' is a conspicuous landmark on several walks along the Medway and in the rich agricultural land spread along and below the hills that rise to the north. And it is this agricultural land that comes under the close attention of students attending KCC's College of Agriculture and Horticulture in a complex of buildings to the south of the village.

At the other end of the walk, West Peckham squats amid fruit-growing country on the lower slopes of the greensand hills which stand heavily clothed with Mereworth Woods a little above the village. A small, but attractive place, it is approached on this outing through acres of strawberry fields, then between hedges to a charming view across the green to the stone-walled parish church, a cottage or two and a weather-boarded pub making a photogenic scene.

Between the two villages there are broad open views, woodlands, a stately country house with its own lake, avenue of cedars and ornate iron gates. There are low-lying fields, orchards and oast houses; a countryside set firm in productivity.

*   *   *

From the heart of Hadlow (1) walk north along the main street (in the direction of Maidstone) until you come to the end of the village. On the right-hand side of the road will be seen a long pond, and a little beyond it The Harrow pub. Just before reaching the pub cross a stile on the left, signposted to Steer's Place and Stallion's Green. The path goes alongside a number of gardens; half-right ahead can be seen Mereworth Woods draped over the hills.

At the end of the gardens continue ahead in the same direction, crossing a number of stiles which take the footpath through a scrubby patch of woodland, then alongside a field with a housing estate seen off to the left. Along this field edge cross another stile by a house, and a few yards later reach a narrow lane at Steer's Place (GR: 631506). Turn left and shortly come to a T junction where you

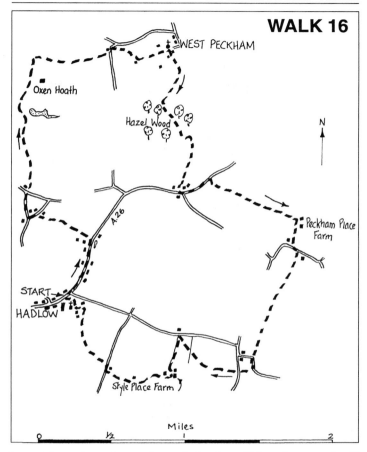

WALK 16

WEST PECKHAM

Oxen Hoath

Hazel Wood

N

A 26

Peckham Place Farm

START

HADLOW

Style Place Farm

Miles

0 ½ 1 2

bear right and wander northwards for about 200 yards to another T junction with a grass triangle and, straight ahead, a footpath marker. Cross a stile, bear right onto a farm track, then turn left and follow as it cuts through a large open field.

Large vistas open all around. The Greensand Ridge sweeps off half-left ahead, and orchards that drape the hills near Plaxtol (Walk

15) can be clearly seen. Directly ahead Mereworth Woods cover hills to the north, but between these hills and the large field through which the track takes us, a grey stone house, Oxen Hoath, studies our approach.

The track eventually leads to a field gate and a stile. Crossing this, pause for a moment to study the country through which you have just walked. It's a large open landscape with a huge sky overall, and May's Folly looming above the trees that screen Hadlow.

The way now lies through parkland to the left of the late 18th-century ragstone manor seen ahead. To the right, and lined with trees, is spread a long attractive lake with a stone-built hump-backed bridge across its narrows. Walk ahead through the parkland, still on a track, though somewhat vague now, and come to a driveway. To the left of the entrance gateway to a cedar avenue go through a metal swing gate and onto the drive, then walk ahead between the cedars and conifers that make a stately avenue approach to the house. Pass another avenue cutting off left, this one of trimmed hedges, and to the right a series of ornate iron gates through which can be seen the well kept gardens of Oxen Hoath.

Continue ahead and pass through another gateway, outside of which the drive forks. Take the left fork, in effect continuing in the same direction for a few yards, then cross a stile on the left (next to a wooden gate) and go half-left up the field to reach a crossing track. Now aim half-right to a stile seen beside a woodland shaw where you join the route of both the Wealdway and Greensand Way.

Over the stile walk along the edge of a field beside the woodland shaw, and at the far end rejoin the farm track/driveway and continue along it. Eventually come to a narrow country road with a lodge house on the left. Turn left, and when the road curves to the right go up a raised footpath beside white railings, and enter a large strawberry field. Walk along its left-hand boundary with more long views across the valley and with May's Folly making a conspicuous landmark.

The boundary leads down to a bungalow. Bear left and walk along a track towards West Peckham church seen beyond a hedge. When the track curves sharply to the right, go through a metal

Oasts at Chiddingstone - the quintessential Kent

At Teston the towpath leads past a lock, a weir and a beautiful medieval bridge. (Walk 28)

The spire of Cowden church beckons across the fields. (Walk 30)

swing gate in the hedge and onto the village green of West Peckham (2). A most attractive scene greets you, with the squat Saxon tower topped by a shingle spire framed by trees making an instinctive subject for a photograph. (All walkers are urged to spare a moment to visit the church before continuing on your way.)

Wander across to The Swan Inn and bear right. Leaving the Wealdway and Greensand Way walk along the track which extends ahead between hedges. It forks after about 130 yards. Bear half-right on a footpath by the side of a small wood, at the end of which go into a field with a woodland on the far side. This is Hazel Wood.

Cross the field and enter Hazel Wood by a stile. A clear footpath leads through, and if you're lucky enough to tackle this walk in springtime, you'll be rewarded by an extravagant ground cover of bluebells - one of the finest displays to be found anywhere. Out of the wood turn left, and shortly after come to a farm track where you bear right. Follow this track across low-lying fields to Goose Green Farm, with its oast houses and complex of converted barns. Bear right and come onto the A26 opposite Leavers Manor Hotel (GR: 646509).

Turn left and walk along the road with care for about 500 yards. It makes a long curve. On the left is a patch of woodland; almost opposite this, on the right-hand side of the road, a stile gives access to a long, narrow field with overhead power lines running the length of it. Walk along the left-hand edge of this field, and at the end continue in the same direction through fields of soft fruit. Come onto a farm drive, rejoining the Wealdway. The drive swings to the right in front of Peckham Place Farm oast houses, and takes you to a narrow road. Turn left for about 100 yards, then bear right on a farm track alongside an orchard, with Crowhurst Farm to the left, its collection of eight oasts adding interest.

Walk straight ahead through the orchard. On the far side find a wooden footbridge over a stream, and continue over a large open field. The route aims to the left of Kent House Farm's oast houses seen on the far side, and joins a country lane about 150 yards from them. Walk down the lane for a short distance until it makes a sharp left-hand bend. Enter the field on the right and walk across it, making for a point about 30 yards to the left of a large grey barn. Here you cross a very narrow lane and walk across the next large field slightly to the right, to gain the far side where the boundary cuts back and to the right. In the corner go through a narrow gap into the next field where you bear half-right, making towards the far right-hand corner where you can see a house. Halfway to the corner cross a driveway and continue in the same direction.

Eventually leave the field at the junction of Court Lane and a drive leading to Style Place Farm (GR: 646494). Turn left and walk down the driveway, bordered by hedges, to reach a complex of converted farm buildings. Bear right in front of the red brick farmhouse to wind between several dwellings and pass the end of a long pond. A track continues, now out among fields, and passes an isolated cottage before eventually coming to another cottage and the Hadlow to Golden Green road.

Turn right along the road for about 30 yards where you will find two sets of metal bars on the left. Go through these and ahead on a metalled footpath that leads all the way to Hadlow. As you wander along the path so May's Folly grows ever higher to dwarf even the church next door. Keep on the main path, wander through a residential area, then resume on the footpath alongside the parish church of St Mary, and out to the main street.

Items of interest:

1: Hadlow. The village is dominated by the tower that is all that remains of one-time Hadlow Court Castle, a large house built in 1779 by Walter Barton May. May was a wealthy and eccentric industrialist who erected the tower as an afterthought. It now makes an interesting landscape feature, all spires and crenellations - an imaginative dwelling. The rest of Hadlow is typically Kentish, with a broad main street, weatherboarded cottages and shops, and a garden countryside all around.

2: West Peckham. A small village in the heart of fruit country. The church of St Dunstan is old and interesting. The tower is Saxon, the north aisle is from the 14th century. There is a curious raised chapel with box pews for the owners of Oxen Hoath, a 17th-century pulpit and a fine screen. And the peace of countless generations held captive among the woodwork.

WALK 17: WEST MALLING - OFFHAM - WEST MALLING

Distance:	5 miles
Maps:	O.S. Pathfinder 1209 'Maidstone' 1:25,000
	O.S. Landranger 188 'Maidstone & The Weald of Kent' 1:50,000
Start:	Manor Park Country Park (GR: 678570)
Access:	The Country Park is located beside A228 just south of West Malling. Nearest railway station: West Malling. Buses from Maidstone
Parking:	At the Country Park (small charge made)
Refreshments:	Pubs, cafés and shops in West Malling; pubs in Offham

On the southern outskirts of West Malling the 52 acres of Manor Park Country Park make a pleasant site for a picnic, or a half-day's outing for children. A long and narrow lake twisting below a steep embankment is its main feature. Trees dip their leaves at its edge, while duck, swan and moorhen busy themselves in their own inimitable style. In a corner between the lake and the road there was once an ice house, where ice from the lake was stored underground for use in the kitchens of Douces Manor opposite. In the little meadow surrounding the ice house wild flowers abound in summer.

The Country Park makes a good starting point for several walks. (Leaflets are usually available.) The following is just one. But please note, if you plan to leave your car there, the Park closes each day at dusk.

This walk is an easy stroll across low-lying fields to Offham, noted for its quintain, or tilting post, that adorns the village green, and is thought to be England's last surviving example of this ancient entertainment. But there's more to the walk than an opportunity to study Offham's quintain, for almost immediately upon leaving the Country Park the path leads past the ruins of a Norman tower. It also takes us through woodland, past pretty cottages to views of the North Downs and open agricultural scenery patterned by orchards, hop gardens and a patchwork of varied crops. In springtime the woods are smoky with bluebells, with wood anemones too in an abundance of white around the lower trunks of the trees.

*   *   *

The walk begins where the access road enters the car park. Here a marker post with red and green paint flashes indicates the start of the footpath, which goes parallel with this road, then leaves the Park through a swing gate next to a row of white cottages opposite St Leonard's Tower (1). Cross the road with care and walk up the track beside the mellow stone tower, and continue along an enclosed footpath through an agricultural landscape.

After about 500 yards come to a country road and cross slightly left to find another track ahead, which goes between a house called Shepherd's Cottage and some farm buildings, and proceeds, enclosed by hedges, as far as Fartherwell Road. Over this enter a field by a stile, turn right and walk along the headland. Coming to a farm drive continue ahead, parallel to the lane, then reaching the end of the cultivated section, bear left and walk along the field edge as far as a small, untidy woodland. A footpath leads through, and emerges in another field. Walk along its right-hand boundary, with a pair of oast houses and Offham church seen two or three fields away.

At the end of the field, just beyond a lone Scots pine, bear left round the headland to the next corner where you veer slightly to the right, pass through a gap and into the neighbouring field. Maintain direction along its left-hand edge. The boundary bends right and left. A few paces later take the footpath heading to the right between

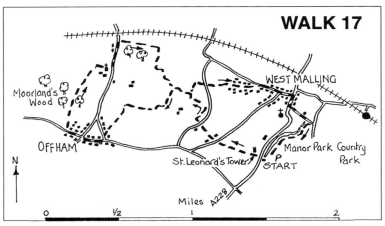

large open fields with the oasts and farm buildings of Godwell seen to the right, and the wall of the North Downs far off.

At the end of this field section come to a crossing track and bear left. When the track curves sharply to the right leave it, and continue ahead. On the far side of the field go over a stile and walk along an enclosed footpath leading to The Red Lion pub in Offham (GR: 659574). A few paces beyond the pub turn right along Teston Road.

Soon come to the village green, with the quintain (2) on the left backed by an assortment of attractive cottages and houses. Maintain direction, pass The Kings Arms and a short distance beyond, turn right into Pepingstraw Close (a playing field on the left). When it bears right, leave the road and walk ahead on an enclosed footpath which takes you into Moorland's Wood. At its entrance the path forks. Take the right-hand option, which may be muddy as it's used by horses.

Coming out of the wood the North Downs look fine ahead, while Offham church tower is seen above the buildings of Church Farm. The footpath leads to a concrete farm road which curves to the right by farm buildings, then slopes uphill and, by the church, joins Church Road. Turn left and wander down this narrow lane. It comes to a row of houses and, just before reaching a railway bridge, you leave it in favour of a track on the right (GR: 662585).

The track narrows to a footpath rising uphill alongside Stubbersdown Wood, a coppice rich in wood anemones. As it ends, come to a junction of paths and bear right along the headland of a large field. On reaching the far side follow the boundary left, and remain with it until you come to the lone Scots pine noted on the outward route. Rejoining the outward route now, go down the left-hand edge of a field for a few paces, and just before the path enters the untidy woodland, break away left on another footpath which enters the neighbouring field. Walk along its left-hand boundary, then bear right at the far corner, and soon come to a stile and a few steps leading down to Fartherwell Road.

Cross this narrow lane directly ahead into the left-hand of two fields. This leads to an enclosed path which goes alongside a playing field. Thereafter a series of obvious paved footpaths takes you through a large residential area to Norman Road, where you

St Leonard's Tower at West Malling was built by the Normans

bear right. This leads to West Street, which in turn takes you directly into the High Street in West Malling (3).

Turn right up the High Street a short distance, then bear left to walk down the narrow Water Lane. Near the bottom of this note the old building of Ewell Monastery on the left. A few yards beyond it go through a wooden swing gate on the right to re-enter Manor Park

Country Park at a junction of paths. Bear sharp right on a stony footpath which soon swings left alongside a stream. You then come to the long and narrow lake which is the Park's main feature, and the path leads back to the car park.

Items of interest:

1: St Leonard's Tower. Managed by English Heritage (not open) this is but one of several structures left in and around West Malling by the Normans. It was built by William the Conqueror's great ecclesiastical architect, Bishop Gundulph, who was also responsible for both cathedral and castle in Rochester. It is supposed that St Leonard's Tower originated as a fortress (some suggest it might have been built as a chapel), but it has had a variety of uses, including that of a prison and a hop store.

2: The Quintain. Tilting is said to have been brought to Britain by the Romans - an entertaining sport, amusing for spectators, but potentially hazardous for those participating. Horsemen would ride at a gallop towards the quintain, or tilting post, from which a sandbag was suspended. At the opposite end to the sandbag was a target, and the whole device pivoted on a post. When the horseman hit the target with his lance, the quintain would spin, threatening to knock the rider from his mount with the whirling sandbag. The sport was popular throughout the Middle Ages, and was revived on Offham green on May Day each year.

3: West Malling. This is a most attractive large village, with a wide street and many fine buildings, including St Mary's Abbey from whose grounds sprays a cascade through an arch in the wall, and the lovely church of St Mary. The 18th-century Douces Manor, which overlooks the lake in Manor Park Country Park, now houses a training centre for an insurance company.

WALK 18: YALDING - HUNTON - BUSTON MANOR - YALDING

Distance:	6½ miles
Maps:	O.S. Pathfinder 1209 'Maidstone' and 1229 'Paddock Wood & Staplehurst' 1:25,000

	O.S. Landranger 188 'Maidstone & The Weald of Kent' 1:50,000
Start:	Yalding church (GR: 698502)
Access:	About 6 miles south-west of Maidstone. The church stands on the right bank of the River Beult, at the south end of Yalding's main street
Parking:	With discretion in Yalding's main street
Refreshments:	Pubs and shops in Yalding

Yalding is a comfortable-looking village set among orchards, fruit fields and streams. It was this countryside of which William Cobbett wrote so enthusiastically in his classic Rural Rides: "The ten miles between Maidstone and Tonbridge I believe to be the very finest, as to fertility and diminutive beauty, in the whole world...There are, on rising grounds, not only hop gardens and beautiful woods, but immense orchards of apples, pears, plums, cherries and filberts, and these, in many cases, with gooseberries and currants and raspberries beneath."

Behind, along the hills, these fertile slopes face the sun. Below, in flat water-meadows, three Kent rivers unite: the Beult, Teise and Medway. Anglers' rivers, they are popular too with canoeists, especially down by the great medieval bridge that spans the Medway beside a weir. Along the village streets are fine cottages and houses, a cluster of oasts, a church with an onion-dome off-centre on its tower, and one of Kent's longest bridges linking two halves of the parish across the River Beult. It's a village with its own individual character, and one that is well worth visiting for itself alone.

This walk explores the two faces of Yalding's countryside. First it heads eastward through the low meadows and fields of the Beult's valley, crossing along the edge of Hunton Park, a short woodland and a series of fields and oast houses. Then it strikes away to the north to climb orchard-clad slopes of the greensand hills, which it then traverses back to Yalding. There are some magnificent broad vistas to highlight the way, framed as they are by a trellis-work of fruit trees. In blossom time it's a vision of rich colour that surrounds the walker, but at all times of the year it's an outing worth tackling.

*   *   *

Begin by walking through Yalding churchyard to the left of the church and, on leaving it, turn right along a track to pass the rear of the local primary school and an extension of the graveyard. The track becomes a footpath that leads to a sports field. Cross along the left-hand edge to a stile, and continue along the boundary of the field beyond, soon passing a red brick house off to your left, and come to a country road (GR: 705498).

Turn right and pass the entrance to a house named Cheveney. At the end of its garden boundary go up four stone steps and over a stile into a field. From here you can see the handsome timber-framed house in its landscaped grounds. The footpath cuts diagonally across the field to the far right-hand corner where a stile brings you onto a drive a little to the left of a white house. Cross the drive and continue ahead on an obvious track going along the edge of several fields. Way off to the left orchards and oast houses are seen sloping up the hillside.

The track leads to Grove Farm. There are several converted farm buildings gathered together here; one an oast house. Wander ahead on the surfaced drive for about 100 yards, then bear left on a track to pass an old barn. About 80 yards along the track turn right along

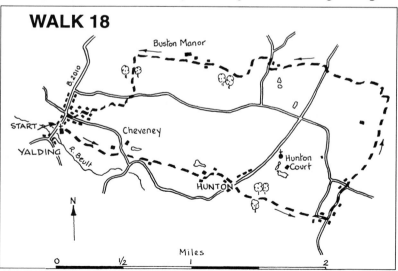

Cheveney, on the outskirts of Yalding

the right-hand edge of an orchard. In the far corner turn right on a short stretch of narrow path, then left by some garages, and soon reach a road in the little village of Hunton (GR: 719494).

Cross the road and go through a swing gate into a meadow with a collection of oast houses and cottages seen a couple of fields away. Wander straight over this meadow to find a stile leading into a wood, about 30 yards to the left of a metal gate. A clear path takes you through this woodland, then out into a corner of Hunton Park (1). Veer half-right to another stile about 100 yards away. As you cross to it, the grey building of Hunton Court is seen way off to the left.

Having crossed out of Hunton Park the way now follows the Park's boundary fence, then beyond, continuing in the same direction towards more oast houses. A series of stiles enables the path to cross two or three fields before bringing it onto a narrow country lane a little to the left of the oast houses (GR: 728490). Turn right and follow the lane round past an early 15th-century timber-framed house. Shortly after this the lane forks. Take the left-hand option, signposted to Linton, and walk along it for about a third of a mile, eventually coming to a T junction beside Foresters Cottages (GR: 733494).

Directly opposite, a public footpath sign directs the route along the side of Elm Corner Cottage. At first this footpath is enclosed by a woodland shaw. Come out of the trees and continue ahead to work your way up the slope between young orchards, passing well to the right of Old Savage Farm. Views are magnificent, and they grow even more expansive as you gain the lip of the ridge. On the way, the spire of Linton church can be seen off to the right, but it is the vast luxury of the Weald that demands constant adoration. At the top of the orchards bear left and follow the boundary until, in a corner, the path leads into a coppice. Almost immediately bear left on another path (the Greensand Way) which hugs the edge of the coppice and eventually slopes into the top edge of the orchard again.

Continue in the same direction along the top edge to the far side of the orchard, then down a steep flight of steps onto a narrow lane. Go up the lane to the right for about 100 yards, then bear left into more orchards. Maintain direction along the hillside, then descend to the lower edge of a bank and walk along the right-hand boundary of the lower orchard.

Enormous views entice you on. Ahead, and a little lower down the slope, you'll see a collection of oasts and converted farm buildings. The path leads to them, swings left then right round the garden boundary, then goes beyond on the driveway to another country lane (GR: 723507). Turn right and walk uphill for about 150 yards to find a track on the left. Go up the track and over a stile, then walk alongside the left-hand hedge. Halfway along the field cross a stile on the left and descend through trees to a lower field where you turn right - still on the Greensand Way. Although you have virtually left orchard country, there remains an uninterrupted vista to enjoy.

When the field breaks away to the right, go downhill through the middle of it, heading south towards the valley. Halfway down come to a crossing track and turn right, now walking towards a woodland. Passing this to your left continue to a large complex of farm buildings; part of the estate of Buston Manor.

Walk through the farmyard and continue ahead on a driveway,

now going downhill onto a track with Buston Manor (2) to your right. The track takes you through the centre of a large field. When you come to a dividing hedge walk along its left-hand side, and soon after reach a cross-track enclosed by trees. This is a bridleway, a sunken track which, turning left, brings you down the slope and out to a country road. Turn right for about 150 yards, then left over a stile to an enclosed footpath which eventually leads round the edge of gardens and out to a residential street. A few yards ahead another path heads left beside the first house and leads directly to another street. Bear right for a few yards, then go left on a footpath starting from a parking bay. It takes you past some almshouses and out near the main street in Yalding (3).

Items of interest:

1: Hunton Park. The Park covers about 100 acres of grassland and woods. In it stands the lovely 13th-century church of St Mary, and the ragstone Hunton Court, a somewhat plain 18th-century manor house once owned by Sir Henry Campbell-Bannerman, one-time Prime Minister.

2: Buston Manor. An L-shaped house standing back from a complex of farm buildings. Although it shows clear evidence of a number of additions and alterations to the original, Buston Manor is another of Kent's many medieval houses which overlooks a great sweep of countryside.

3: Yalding. Divided by the River Beult, which is spanned by a long, 15th-century bridge, the northern half of the village is instantly attractive. The main street is lined with houses and cottages bearing a mixture of materials and architectural styles, yet the appearance is altogether pleasing. The well proportioned church of St Peter and St Paul looks grand from without and within. A little south of the village a magnificent medieval ragstone bridge spans the Medway beside a lock and a weir.

WALK 19: LINTON - BOUGHTON MONCHELSEA PLACE - LINTON

Distance:	5 miles
Maps:	O.S. Pathfinder 1229 'Paddock Wood & Staplehurst' and 1209 'Maidstone' 1:25,000
	O.S. Landranger 188 'Maidstone & The Weald of Kent' 1:50,000
Start:	Linton church (GR: 755502)
Access:	Via A229 south of Maidstone, about ¹/₂ mile south of B2163 crossroads
Parking:	Public car park just north of the church
Refreshments:	Pub in Linton

The village of Linton enjoys a sun-trap of a position on the southern slopes of the Greensand Ridge about 3¹/₂ miles south of Maidstone. And what a position! There's a huge view overlooking the Weald, with the River Beult curling sedately at the foot of the slope. The panorama includes uncountable acres of orchard and fruit field as though this were one vast market garden. The garden of England.

To the east stretch greenswards of parkland. Then more orchards and more parklands and fruit fields and orchards again. To the west sweeps a bewildering complexity of fruit trees. Orchard after orchard, immaculately pruned, regimentally set along the hills; trim, neat, admirably laid out. Oast houses, farms, a few barns and tile-hung cottages punctuate these bountiful acres. In the valley below, the glint of sun on water betrays the river and one or two recently created farm reservoirs.

This walk is a joy; gentle and undemanding, with only one short uphill section. But of course it comes into its own in blossom time. Then there's a delirium of colour and fragrance, with bees thundering among the orchard trees, and grand views framed by nature's seasonal burst of extravagance.

*   *   *

Wander through the churchyard of St Nicholas heading east, away from the road, and enter the grounds of Linton Park (1) on an enclosed footpath. Cross a drive (the massive white house can be

109

seen to the right) and maintain direction following the route of the Greensand Way. This leads behind a ragstone house, crosses Loddington Lane, passes a converted oast house, and then views open over the Wealden expanse. Orchards line the hills and the valley, while the southern slopes are dressed also with fields of soft fruit.

Then the stumpy tower of Boughton Monchelsea church is seen ahead, and as you draw near, so too is the extensive, farm-like entrance to Boughton Place (2), although the house itself will not be seen for some time. The path forks. Bear left. (The alternative reaches a lane near the church, from whose door a magnificent view overlooks Boughton deer park.) Our path curves round to cross Church Lane and continues through a small patch of coppice woodland.

Out of the woodland cross a meadow, go over a drive and into a hilltop field. This leads to a second large field sloping down to the Weald. On reaching the far boundary turn right and walk downhill, with an orchard on the left and Wierton Place seen beyond it. Continue down the slope, passing a dutch barn in the neighbouring field, then downhill still for another 100 yards to find a stile on the right leading into Boughton Park.

The park is lovely. At the foot of the slope a small tree-encircled lake flows into another, smaller, pool. Bulrushes line the interlocking

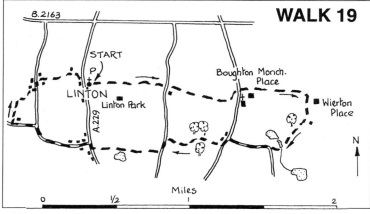

stream, and birds dart to and fro among them. Off to the right, behind a high fence, fallow deer may be seen grazing, while on the far side of the park Boughton Monchelsea church and Boughton Place stand on the crown of the slope. It's a tranquil scene - just right for a picnic.

Go down the slope to pass along the left-hand edge of the smaller pool, then strike away half-right to a metal field gate and stile in the boundary fence (GR: 774495). Leave the park here and bear right along a lane for about a third of a mile, enjoying views through the deer fence and up the sweep of parkland to the church and ragstone mansion. The lane comes to a T junction. Turn left, and after passing Church Barn Farm - a barn conversion - bear right on a footpath running alongside the boundary hedge. Walk down the field to its far corner where a plank footbridge crosses a ditch. Immediately over this go left into a woodland that is magnificent with primrose, celandine, wood anemone and bluebells in spring. Marker posts direct the path through, winding left, then right alongside a fence.

Beyond the woodland go down a grass slope, over a brook and into an orchard. Walk through the orchard and onto a lane by way of a stile next to a field gate. Turn left. There is another woodland on your right which ends at a fenced enclosure. Beyond this bear right on a footpath leading into Linton Park.

Walk straight ahead alongside old fenceposts. Way off to the right can be seen the great white mansion of Linton Park, a huge building set among trees and shrubs. Pass alongside a lake with trees around it. On the far side of the parkland join the A229 below Linton village. Cross the road with care, turn right and take the first turning on the left: Wheelers Lane (GR: 755495).

At first this is a residential street, but houses soon give way to orchards, and a view west along the slopes of the greensand hills. At Toke Farm the lane curves and through orchards a fine view may be had to Linton church. When the lane forks bear left into Barnes Lane. Just beyond Bramley Cottage cross a stile on the right and walk uphill along the edge of an orchard. Come to another stile in the fence ahead. Over this bear right, slanting uphill towards farm buildings. Keeping these to your left come to a lane guarded by a very high hedge of cypresses. Turn left and wander along the lane until the cypress hedge/windbreak ends at a farm drive. A footpath sign indicates the way to Linton church. Follow the drive as it winds between orchards with a superb panorama. Caught in the sun this curving hillside is a wonderland of colour and artistry; an immense patchwork of orchards - the fertile land put to productive use.

After passing Little Court, a solitary pink house on the left, climb a flight of steps and continue into the car park of The Bull Inn, almost opposite Linton church.

Items of interest:

1: Linton Park. The house was built in the 1730s by Robert Mann on a magnificent site overlooking the Weald. As Horace Walpole described it, so it is: "...like the citadel of Kent, the whole county its garden".

2: Boughton Place. Set beside the church of St Peter that has, surely, one of the finest views from its door of any church in the county, Boughton Place was built in 1567 from locally quarried ragstone. (The same quarries supplied stone from which Westminster Abbey was built.) The house is open to the public on set days during the summer.

WALK 20: LEEDS - BROOMFIELD - LEEDS CASTLE - LEEDS

Distance:	2³/₄ miles
Maps:	O.S. Pathfinder 1210 'Harrietsham' 1:25,000
	O.S. Landranger 188 'Maidstone & The Weald of Kent' 1:50,000
Start:	Leeds church (GR: 826534)
Access:	On B2163 cutting south from A20, 4¹/₂ miles east of Maidstone
Parking:	With discretion in the village. (A notice in the church car park states it is for villagers and users of church and school.)
Refreshments:	Pubs in Leeds village

Although this is the shortest walk in the book, it's highly recommended for the views it gives of what has been described as "the loveliest castle in the world". Leeds Castle sits on two small islands in a lake formed by the little River Len, among parkland and stately trees. An almost perfect scene. It is, quite justifiably, very popular with visitors, and anyone who follows this route through the grounds will, I'm sure, be eager to return to visit the castle itself at a later date. (There is no access to the castle or facilities within the grounds, for walkers on the route described. But you are urged to come back another time, by the official entrance, to enjoy the rest of this enchanting place.)

Leeds village, where the walk begins, is a pretty community of winding streets lined with ageing timber-framed or Kentish weatherboarded cottages. There is some fine countryside around, and a number of footpaths that explore it. The walk described below is the best of the bunch.

* * *

Walk through Leeds churchyard and out at the right-hand corner by way of a swing gate leading into a meadow. Wander towards the left-hand side of the 15th-century Battel Hall, go over a narrow lane and enter a second meadow. Aiming half-right to a group of four large trees you will come to a stile, over which you enter the parkland that contains Leeds Castle (1), seen to the left. Maintain direction, cross a driveway and come to another stile in a fence

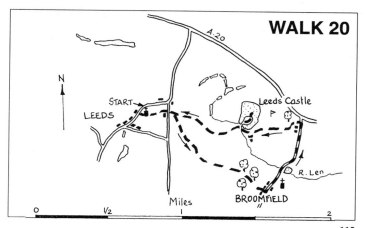

separating the parkland from a field.

Over the stile follow the fence ahead, still with Leeds Castle seen in the valley. At the end of the field a gate takes you into a plantation, beyond which you continue alongside a hedge, then a woodland, before entering the hamlet of Broomfield by some cottages (GR: 838525).

Turn left and walk through the hamlet, which consists of a handful of cottages and a grey stone-built church standing back on the right. At the entrance to the church approach, note St Margaret's Well beside the lane.

Follow the lane for about 1/2 mile, crossing the River Len that eases from a rather overgrown stretch of lake on the right; and eventually draw level with a pair of lodge cottages at the entrance gates to the Leeds Castle estate. Continue on the lane until, just before reaching a T junction, you go through a fence on the left to re-enter the grounds of Leeds Castle.

Note: It is essential to keep to the public right of way described through the Castle grounds. Please do not stray from the route.

The way takes you down some steps to the edge of a golf course, then veers left, following waymarks among trees, to reach a driveway. Bear right and walk along the drive which cuts through parkland. As you proceed so the castle appears quite magnificent in its lake. Cross the causeway by the castle entrance and bear left up a continuing driveway, soon passing a small car park on the left. Go through a gateway and then follow marker posts leading across the parkland on the right-hand side of the drive. As you do so, note the splendid scene over your right shoulder: a sweep of cropped grass, a landscaped woodland with a pool and river contained within, and the mellow stonework of the castle itself dazzling in the lake. Idyllic.

Wandering from one marker post to the next you will come to a swing gate which takes you out of the parkland and into a cricket ground. Continue ahead to another swing gate on the far side, and beyond it through a small meadow. This brings you to the lane beside Battel Hall where you rejoin the outward route back to Leeds church.

Items of interest:

1: Leeds Castle. There has been a castle here, in one form or another, since A.D. 857 when King Ethelbert's Chief Minister, Ledian, constructed a wooden fortress on the Len. When the Normans arrived, they replaced timber with stone, and over the many centuries that followed the castle grew to the beautiful mellow structure we gaze on today. For some 300 years it was owned by the crown. It was the home of Catherine of Aragon, first wife of Henry VIII, and Elizabeth I, Henry's daughter, was imprisoned there before she was made queen. In the 17th-century French prisoners were held in the castle. It was restored 200 years later, and thanks to a Trust set up in 1974 on the death of Lady Baillie (who bought it in 1926), both castle and grounds are now open daily to the public.

Eden Valley and The Medway

Bounded by the Greensand Ridge to the north and High Wealden hills of East Sussex to the south, the valleys of the Eden and young Medway are a delight of meadowlands and woods. Their rivers add something special to a colourful corner, full of interest, rich in character, deep-bedded in history. Streams writhe in sunken channels, their banks massed with wild garlic in springtime, their shadowed spinneys swamped with bluebells, their hedgerows shoulder high in the white lace of cow parsley, their great parklands ablaze with rhododendrons and azaleas.

In truth, this is but one small part of the Weald, but it is such a significant part that it deserves a section of its own. From the greensand belvederes of Crockham Hill and Ide Hill, it is sometimes difficult to believe that the land spread below has been settled and tended for nearly two thousand years. But man has been thoughtful here, his care of the land and its landscapes has been guided by love, so that in any one of a number of corners we find that the Eden Valley has become a veritable Garden of Eden.

Ancient farms lie scattered about this generous countryside, as do stately homes rich in history and romance: Hever Castle, Penshurst Place, Chiddingstone Castle. There are manor houses secluded among leafy bowers, or standing away from prying eyes behind long walls that hide their parklands from the outside world. There are villages of undisputed charm like Cowden, Chiddingstone and Penshurst. Hamlets that gaze across a folding wonderland of greenery, as does Hoath Corner, far from anywhere, and there are gems of surprise waiting to be discovered on hilltop and in woodland to reward the wanderer of the long-established trails that allow by far the best method of exploring the region.

The Medway is Kent's major river. It rises over the border in Sussex - one of its sources being a peat bog on Ashdown Forest - but soon enters the county to impose its own quiet character. Several branches unite outside Groombridge and flow northwards via Ashurst and below Fordcombe, snaking through meadows before coming to Penshurst, there to be swollen by the Eden. At Penshurst the Medway then bears eastward on its journey to Tonbridge, and from Tonbridge to Maidstone as a navigable waterway of locks and fine bridges, with a pleasant towpath walk of 16 miles.

The Eden is more stream than river, but its valley lacks nothing in interest. And there's Kent Water too, the stream that marks the county boundary just west of Cowden to the flat meadowlands below Fordcombe. Again, this stream lures the walker into a heartland of countryside, into a dream-world of flowers and birdsong. Some of Kent's best walking is to be had alongside it.

In summer the lanes are busy with cars and coaches making the pilgrimage to various castles and extravagant country houses. Yet take to the footpaths and the benevolence of the countryside will embrace you with its peace. Many of our walks will lead, too, to these historic sites, to enable the walker to share in this heritage. But better by far, it is, to be wandering over hill and through dappled wood where the real England that predates even the centuries-old buildings we treasure so much, can still be experienced.

In the Eden Valley and along the Medway no walker need ever run short of ideas or inspiration.

*   *   *

WALK 21: FOUR ELMS - WINKHURST GREEN (BOUGH BEECH RESERVOIR) - FOUR ELMS

Distance:	4 miles
Maps:	O.S. Pathfinder 1228 'Tonbridge & Edenbridge' 1:25,000
	O.S. Landranger 188 'Maidstone & The Weald of Kent' 1:50,000
Start:	Four Elms (GR: 468483)
Access:	The village is on a crossroads formed by B269 and B2042. About 2 miles north-east of Edenbridge
Parking:	In a lay-by on B269 opposite Four Elms church
Refreshments:	Pub in Four Elms

This short walk should be of interest to bird watchers, since the corner of Bough Beech Reservoir it visits is a nature reserve, and a nearby lagoon has

117

become a noted breeding site for a variety of duck and geese. The walk also leads to a converted oast house at Winkhurst Green that has been turned into an information centre manned by volunteers from the Kent Trust for Nature Conservation (KTNC), with some interesting displays telling of the changes that occurred when the East Surrey Water Company flooded a valley in the late 1960s to create the reservoir. Upstairs, in the oast's roundel, a museum devoted to the hop industry has been established. If the centre is open when you arrive (summers only, on Wednesdays and at weekends), you are urged to include a visit as part of the walk.

* * *

Facing the church (on the Tonbridge road) turn left towards The Four Elms pub. Immediately before reaching a small stream cross a stile beside a field gate on the right. Walk across the meadow with the stream to your left, and come to a plank footbridge over a drainage ditch. Now go diagonally across this field towards the far right-hand corner where you pass through a gap into an adjacent field. Follow the left-hand hedgerow towards a field gate with a stile beside it. Continue ahead, but when you reach another field gate on your left, turn right, go through a gap and then bear left to a stile

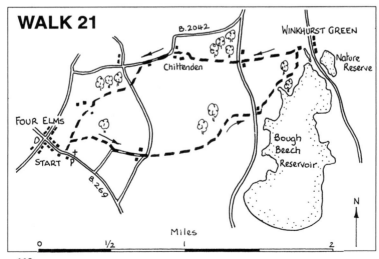

which will bring you to a lane at an elbow bend (GR: 474483). Bear left and walk up the lane towards a farm.

Come to a T junction with a house called Little Blackmoor on the right, and Roodlands Farm on the left. Bear left, and a few paces later you will see a metal field gate on the right, with a stile immediately to the right of that. Cross the stile, bear left, then wander along the edge of the field, with views to far-off hills and dipping woodlands.

At the end of the field you come to a woodland shaw. Bear right for a few paces, then left through a gap and walk along the side of the shaw which, in springtime, is bright with flowers, with buds in the trees, birds everywhere and plenty of signs of activity from foxes and rabbits. On reaching a metal field gate in the hedge ahead, go through it and continue along the edge of the next field, with a more substantial wood on your left. This is Chittenden Wood.

Towards the end of this large field the wood finishes. Go over a stile in the top left-hand corner into a clump of trees, then immediately turn right to cross a footbridge over a little brook. Directly ahead can be seen the buildings of Hilders Farm. There is no clear footpath in this field, but the direction to take is off to the left towards the far hedge. As you approach it you will see a metal hurdle in lieu of a stile. This allows a crossing of the hedgerow. Over this turn right and walk along the edge of the field. On entering a second field bear slightly right through a gap, then resume direction, now with a hedge on the left, and soon reach a country road opposite the triple-gabled Hilders Farm Cottage (GR: 489486). Nearby stretch the waters of Bough Beech Reservoir (1).

Turn right in front of the house, and on coming to the end of its garden, cross a stile on the left and follow the enclosed path beyond. It leads to within a few yards of the reservoir, makes a sharp left-hand bend and crosses a stile into a large field. Follow a line of power cables stretching across this field, and on coming to the corner of a wood branch away diagonally half-right towards a stile in the hedge. To your right is the reservoir, here appearing as a natural lake, with little bays and trees growing down to the water's edge.

Draw level with a woodland on your right. This is a nature reserve, and the footpath follows round its edge. At the end of the wood bear left over a stile, and cross a narrow field to another stile in a line of trees. Ahead, a couple of fields away, can be seen the oast house of the Bough Beech Centre at Winkhurst Green (GR: 495494). The walk leads directly to it.

Note: If you are interested in bird watching, walk along the oast house driveway to a country road. Then bear right for a short distance to gain the causeway from which ornithologists spend hours observing wildlife in the reservoir to the right, or in the lagoons to the left of the road. Herons can almost be guaranteed, standing in the shallows in search of fish. Assorted duck and geese breed here, and numerous waders will also be seen.

Returning to our circular walk, leave the oast house and go back through the swing gate behind it. Now walk uphill along the right-hand edge of a sloping field. At the top cross a stile and continue along a track as far as a country road reached between two houses. Cross the road, go over a stile directly ahead, and walk down a track with a wood on your right. This eventually crosses a brook and approaches Chittenden Farm. Before reaching the farm, however, the track comes to a field gate, with a metal field gate beside it, and a third field gate to the right. Go through the right-hand gate and walk along the left-hand boundary of the field until you find a stile and a plank footbridge in a corner. Cross these among trees, go ahead, then bear left on an enclosed footpath that leads alongside the buildings of Chittenden Farm. Shortly after, curve leftwards to avoid a hedge surrounding the garden of a house on the right, then slope down to a road (GR: 481494). Turn left and walk along it for about 400 yards.

Pass Little Chittenden, with Piggott's Wood on the right. About 150 yards beyond the house there's a pond on the left with a gate and stile leading into a field. Bear half-right across the field and pass through a gap in a partial hedge. Maintain direction towards double poles that carry power cables. On reaching them a stile takes you onto another lane. Cross to a stile opposite and walk ahead down the edge of a large field, with a wood on your right. When the wood finishes continue ahead down the edge of the field, and go left round the boundary of Holmwood Place. Coming to the bottom of the field cross a stile and plank footbridge into a second field near a brick building which looks like a small barn, but is a cowshed. Pass to the right of the cowshed, following a winding stream which leads to another stile. Over this continue ahead to another plank footbridge - the same plank footbridge that began the walk. Cross the field to gain the road once more in Four Elms.

Items of interest:

1: Bough Beech Reservoir. An extensive sheet of water created in the late 1960s by East Surrey Water Company who flooded part of a valley. One or two of the buildings that stood in the valley were dismantled piece by piece and re-erected at the Weald and Downland Museum, Singleton, in Sussex. The reservoir has taken on a natural appearance for the majority of its area, but there is limited access to it. At the northern end there's a bird reserve, safe from disturbance by sailing enthusiasts. Bird watchers congregate on the causeway between the reservoir and the special lagoons created to encourage wildfowl. The site is now important as a wintering place for geese, and as a breeding site for various ducks. Volunteers from the KTNC man an information centre in a nearby converted oast house - recommended.

WALK 22: LEIGH - FLETCHER'S GREEN - LEIGH

Distance:	6 miles
Maps:	O.S. Pathfinder 1228 'Tonbridge & Edenbridge' 1:25,000
	O.S. Landranger 188 'Maidstone & The Weald of Kent' 1:50,000
Start:	Leigh church (GR: 549466)
Access:	Via B2027 about 3 miles west of Tonbridge. Nearest railway station: Leigh
Parking:	With discretion by Leigh village green - but not on it
Refreshments:	Pubs in Leigh and Fletcher's Green. Shops in Leigh

Parkland, woods and rolling farmland are the ingredients of this walk. There are expansive views, attractive farms, clear winding streams and a remote hamlet to capture your imagination. In winter some sections are bound to be muddy, but for the remainder of the year - except following a spell of prolonged rain - this is a walk of great charm.

Leigh is a busy village strung around a large green, with the church of St Mary opposite - part of an attractive scene with an arched gateway and lodge at the entrance to Hall Place drive. Hall Place is a red-brick mansion built in the style of the Tudors, with an extensive lake, hidden from the village, but seen from our walk.

*   *   *

From the B2027 on the northern edge of the village go up the slope beside the entrance to Leigh church on a footpath signposted to

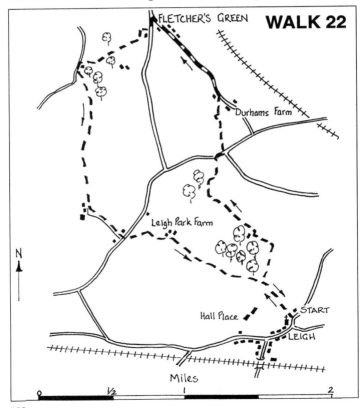

WALK 22

FLETCHER'S GREEN

Durhams Farm

Leigh Park Farm

N

Hall Place

START

LEIGH

Miles

0   ½   1   2

Lower Street and Weald. This goes to the side of a timber-framed house, with the lodge and gateway to Hall Place on your left. Walk ahead beside a wall to a swing gate, and through this down the left-hand edge of a large field beside a fence with Hall Place parkland beyond it. At the bottom of the field come to a woodland corner where the path forks. Take the right-hand option over a stile and a footbridge, and wander ahead beside the wood. When this cuts back to the left, continue ahead over the field bay and so reach a broad woodland shaw. Wander through it and come to a farm track where you turn left. This leads to a cottage, but just before coming to it bear right in front of a garage. Soon after turn left on a track heading into the woods. In a few yards the track forks. Take the left branch, in effect continuing in the same direction through the woods.

On emerging from the trees go ahead slightly to the right, making for what appears to be the right-hand edge of a woodland on the far side of a large field. On reaching it, however, this proves to be a shaw projecting from a wood. Walk down the right-hand side of this shaw, then continue round the headland of the field, with the wood to your left. In it there are many wild cherry trees, and their blossom makes a halo of confetti in springtime. When the wood ends continue in the same direction, now beside another shaw and still following the field edge. Shortly after passing a silted-up pond, the field juts back to form a shallow bay, and in the corner you will find a single plank footbridge over a ditch, leading into a narrow field. Walk up its left-hand side, then over a stile come onto a lane (GR: 542485).

Turn right and walk along the lane a short distance until you come to another breaking away to the right. A few paces beyond this junction find a stile on the left beside a field gate. Over this bear half-right and walk across the field to the far corner where there's another stile by a gate. Cross the next field to a stile found about 30 yards to the left of a metal field gate, then walk across the narrow section of the field ahead, and bear left round its boundary with a stream winding in a deep cut below. In a few yards reach yet another field gate. Through this bear left, cross another stile and walk across a field aiming for the far side about 30 yards to the right of a tile-hung cottage. Here a final stile leads onto a narrow country road where you turn left.

Keep on the lane for almost a mile to reach a T junction at Fletcher's Green; a collection of cottages, houses and a farm (GR: 533501). (This junction is just off the recommended 1:25,000 map.) Bear left towards The Chequer Tree pub. Before reaching it, however, turn right at a field entrance on a track that veers slightly left. Walk alongside the right-hand hedgerow to reach a double stile. Do not cross, but instead turn left along the edge of the field to the far corner. Here you will find another stile on the right. Cross this and maintain direction over the next field towards the left-hand edge of a small group of trees where another stile leads into the next field. Continue in the same direction and come to a farm track. Cross to another stile. Over this bear half-left and walk to the left of a solitary oak tree, beyond which you come to the top corner of a woodland and another stile leading into it. Follow the path through and out the other side, where you go slightly left of centre over a sloping field, across another stile and down through a second woodland. At the bottom of this come onto a lane beside Brook Cottage (GR: 526496).

Turn left, walk past the cottage and along the lane for a few yards, then take an enclosed footpath on the left. It climbs among scrub and trees and along the top edge of some woods (not shown on the O.S. map). These are private, but the path traces along their edge and emerges over a stile to a large field.

Walk straight across this field to a stile found slightly to the left of a large oak in a line of trees. Continue in the same direction to a set of wooden bars on the far boundary of the next field. This is a large rolling countryside, with broad views to distant hills with woods and smaller clumps of trees breaking the sweep of far-off meadow; a peaceful, tranquil landscape, and a sheer delight to be wandering through on a bright day of sunshine and fluffs of cloud.

Having crossed the wooden bars you then go over the next field towards another set of bars beside a field gate. On reaching these you have a view to distant oast houses of Coppings Farm half-left across two or three fields. There is a path to them, but ours leads straight on, still following the same direction as before, while another goes to the right, to Charcott and Chiddingstone Causeway. A stile beneath a large oak tree in the opposite hedge directs the path over a footbridge and into the next field. Here bear slightly right and

Leigh, the church and lodge gate at the entrance to Hall Place

walk across to another stile to the right of a pond. Cross this and follow the right-hand edge of a field towards another pond found among sparse trees. Bear left and soon locate a stile in the field corner. Now go ahead to reach a row of cottages near Wickhurst Farm. Walk past the cottages and in a few yards come to a junction of drives. Turn left and walk down the driveway to a road (GR: 531476).

On the opposite side of the road cross a stile and turn left, then wander along the field boundary as far as a metal field gate giving onto a concrete farm drive. Bear right towards Leigh Park Farm. The drive curves to the left, then makes a sharp left-hand bend round a double oast beside a pond. A few yards after this turn right through a field gate and walk ahead along the edge of three fields until you come to woods. A stile leads into them, and a clear path takes you through delightful mixed woods, with conifers and deciduous varieties, and a large number of rhododendrons too. After a while the path becomes enclosed by fences and runs along the right-hand edge of the woods, with Hall Place seen to the right standing above its large lake.

On coming to a metal swing gate go through it and head up the right-hand edge of a large field leading back to Leigh (1) on the path first trodden on the outward route.

Items of interest:

1: Leigh. The village is not as old as at first it appears, although there has been a settlement here for many centuries. The church of St Mary dates from the 13th century, but many of the Tudor-style cottages along the main street were built in the Victorian era by Samuel Morley, who had Hall Place built too, in 1871. It stands in 200 acres of parkland.

WALK 23: HEVER - CHIDDINGSTONE - HEVER

Distance:	5 miles
Maps:	O.S. Pathfinder 1228 'Tonbridge & Edenbridge' 1:25,000
	O.S. Landranger 188 'Maidstone & The Weald of Kent' 1:50,000
Start:	Hever church (GR: 476448)
Access:	By minor road about 2½ miles south-east of Edenbridge. Nearest railway station: Hever (1 mile)
Parking:	Near the church
Refreshments:	Pubs in Hever and Chiddingstone. Tearoom in Chiddingstone

This walk is especially fine in spring and autumn. In springtime the woods are fresh, colourful and lively with birdsong. Several damp patches of woodland and streamside are swamped with wild garlic, and bluebells too. In autumn the beeches throw a golden carpet underfoot and overhead, an umbrella of yellow and soft ochre tinged with green. Pheasants scamper heavy-bellied along our footpaths, while the gentle landscapes hold an atmosphere of tranquillity that owes much to the history of this corner of old England.

That history is inevitably linked with the story of Anne Boleyn and Henry VIII, for Hever Castle was the childhood home of this mother of the first Elizabeth. She grew up among these meadows and trees. She would have walked the few yards from the castle to the church, where later her father was buried, and Henry would no doubt have ridden the byways here, perhaps with a hawk upon his wrist. Today the castle attracts visitors by the thousand, but the footpaths are empty save for the business of pheasants and squirrels.

Chiddingstone is hardly less interesting than Hever. Its castle may not have the history nor style of Hever's, but the collection of handsome Tudor cottages that line the street opposite the church help make this one of Kent's best loved villages.

Between Hever and Chiddingstone there are beechwoods (in part damaged by storm) with outcrops of greensand in them. And beyond Chiddingstone a charming stretch of countryside lost in a period of time that bears little relationship with today's headlong pursuit of technology. Our walk takes us into history, and along footpaths and beside streams that breathe a spirit of unhurried calm.

* * *

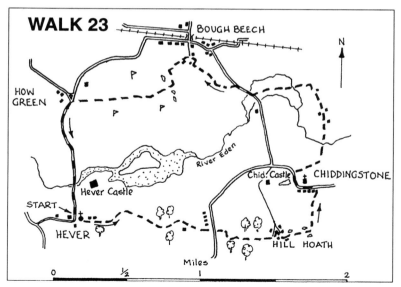

The first section, as far as Hill Hoath, is waymarked as the Eden Valley Walk. It goes through the churchyard of St Peter's in Hever (1), and down to the bottom end of the graveyard where an enclosed footpath passes along the edge of a small woodland (wild garlic and bluebells in spring), and continues past the gardens of a row of cottages.

After a while you can just see Hever Castle's lake some way ahead to the left. Soon after, the path, still enclosed by fences, curves to the right alongside a private road. A wooden footbridge takes you over the road and continues ahead, now with storm-thinned woods on the left. Eventually come to a small gate (the road is barred by a locked field gate), where you go through, cross the road half-right, then walk along the left-hand side of a fence boundary. Go through a stand of pine trees and continue beside the fence until you come to a country road well to the right of a row of four houses (GR: 491447).

Cross the road directly ahead to a stile in the corner of a field. Beyond this the way is led by fences, and with a stream below to the right. Again, there will be the pungent smell of wild garlic in springtime. After about 120 yards cross a stile leading into the field on the right, and soon after this, cross a footbridge on the left which takes you into a coppice woodland. The path rises through the coppice and brings you to a high deer fence which directs you nearly all the way to Hill Hoath. (This fencing is to be regretted as it has devalued some of the pleasures of this part of the walk.)

Passing through storm-damaged beechwoods the path has been deeply cut through outcrops of greensand, with tree roots clawing over it, and with a hole cleft in the left-hand wall which allows a view out to more rocks and trees and the slope sweeping down. Before the '87 storm there was a lovely beechwood glade with the outcrops forming a horseshoe to one side. Now, alas, just a memory.

Beyond the rocks the trail leads to Hill Hoath. Walk ahead between the houses, passing Withers, an old timber-framed house on the left. At a crossing drive/road turn right and walk up the slope towards Hill Hoath Farm. Bear left by farm buildings, with cottages to your left. Keep to the left of a dutch barn following the line of a

Scotney Castle, one of the most romantic sites in all Kent

Secluded in a soft downland valley, Crundale gathers the peace of the hills. (Walk 36)
Hastingleigh, on a neat circuit beginning on Wye Downs. (Walk 37)

fence, and reach a pond. Immediately beyond this the Eden Valley Walk bears right, but we leave it and continue straight ahead, through a scrub area between two more scruffy ponds, over a stile and then bear left. The path now leads up a slope, with the tower of Chiddingstone church rising out of the hidden country beyond. A series of stiles then directs the footpath from the crown of the slope to the single street of Chiddingstone (2). Turn left and walk into the village (GR: 501452).

Walk through Chiddingstone, bearing right between the church and pub, and follow the road to the northern end of a lake across which Chiddingstone Castle is seen. Immediately after crossing the end of the lake go through a metal swing gate on the right, leading into a field with a pond in it. Fine views ahead to the greensand hills. Walk down the right-hand side of the field, seeing the handsome red-brick house called Gilwyns with St Mary's church behind it off to your right; a picturesque sight.

Following the right-hand hedgerow down the field come to a gap leading into the next field. Through this bear half-left aiming towards the left-hand corner of a woodland. Chiddingstone Causeway church can be seen in the distance. On reaching the corner of the wood join another path coming from Chiddingstone. Turn left and follow this across a field to a concrete footbridge over the River Eden. An enclosed footpath continues ahead to a driveway next to a tile-hung house, Somerden Green. Walk up the driveway, passing one or two more houses on the left, and eventually a cottage on the right. This is North Cottage, with an old water pump in the garden.

Just beyond North Cottage cross a stile on the left and walk across the field, enjoying delightful views over a rolling countryside, with Chiddingstone church and castle once more seen way off to the left.

The footpath leads to another bridge crossing the River Eden. Keeping in the same direction walk ahead across the long field beyond the river, and eventually join a country road by way of a stile next to a field gate. Turn right, and in a few paces cross the River Eden again. Continue along the road for about 100 yards, then come to a pair of metal field gates on the left. Go through the second of these, and walk up the left-hand edge of the field for about 100 yards, then bear left through a gap into the next field. On the left is a war-time pillbox.

Turn right immediately and go up the right-hand side of the sloping field. Near the brow of the hill go through another gap into the next field ahead, and walk along its left-hand edge, making towards a small barn. Swing to the right in front of it, and pass a metal field gate on your left. Shortly before some cottages bear left on an enclosed footpath leading to a driveway near a pond.

Note: Those in need of refreshment should turn right and follow the driveway/track for about 250 yards to The Wheatsheaf pub in Bough Beech.

Cross the track, go through a field gate and turn left down the edge of the field. On reaching the end cross a stile into Hever Golf Course. Bear left and walk down a path that will lead across the golf course. The path is clear and adequately waymarked; the course landscaped with ponds and streams and with a parkland quality about it (so different to the countryside experienced when walking the path described in the 1st edition of this guide). After walking about two-thirds of a mile across it, the broad sandy path swings to the right towards the clubhouse. At this point leave the golfing path, cross a stile ahead and follow a hedgerow as far as a road at How Green (GR: 475462). Turn left and walk down the road, with care, to Hever.

Items of interest:

1: Hever. The glory of Hever belongs to the church and the castle. Side by side they stand among trees and parkland, with the pub opposite and farmland all around. Built in the 13th century by William de Hever as a fortified farmhouse, the castle was given further fortifications a hundred years later. The Bullens (as the Boleyn family was originally known) took the castle in the 15th century and there Anne was born. There came Henry to court her. But the happiness of Hever was short-lived, for in 1536 Anne and her brother, George, were executed by Henry's orders, and their father Thomas died of a broken heart two years later. On his death Henry gave Hever Castle to his fourth wife, Anne of Cleves, from whom he had recently been divorced. She retained it for 17 years.

From the outside this little moated castle looks much as it would have done in Anne Boleyn's day, but inside major restoration work was carried out by wealthy American, William Waldorf Astor, who bought the estate in 1903. Not only did he restore the interior, but he built a Tudor-style row of cottages, created ornamental gardens and, with 2,000 workmen, laid out a 35-acre lake. The castle and grounds are open to the public.

The church of St Peter is another magnificent country place of worship that owes its origins to craftsmen of another age. Much of it belongs to the 14th and 15th centuries; it has a shingle spire, a Jacobean pulpit, a lectern and iron screens made by a local blacksmith a hundred years ago. And it has some truly splendid brasses. One is of Anne Boleyn's father dressed in the robes of a Knight of the Garter, his feet resting on a griffin; another is of Margaret Cheyne who was buried in 1419. She has angels at her head and a dog at her feet. The Henry VIII Inn opposite the church is another fine old timbered building, originally known as The Bull.

2: Chiddingstone. A rarity, is Chiddingstone. Its single street of Tudor houses is owned by the National Trust. A very small village, but a splendid one with its half-timbered buildings overhanging the street opposite the huge church of St Mary's. The church dates from around the 14th century, but was rebuilt in the 17th century following a fire. Next to The Castle Inn (it has been an inn since 1730) stand the great iron gates that lead to Chiddingstone Castle, formerly High Street House. It was never really a castle, but a Tudor manor that was almost completely demolished in 1679 by Henry Streatfeild, who then set about replacing the original with a mansion of red brick. A century later the red brick mansion was encased in stone and given little turrets and battlements. More towers were added later to achieve the rather unlovely appearance of a Gothic 'castle' we see today.

WALK 24: PENSHURST - CHIDDINGSTONE - PENSHURST

Distance:	4½ miles
Maps:	O.S. Pathfinder 1228 'Tonbridge & Edenbridge' 1:25,000
	O.S. Landranger 188 'Maidstone & The Weald of Kent' 1:50,000

Start:	Penshurst (GR: 527438)
Access:	Via B2176 about 4½ miles south-west of Tonbridge. Nearest railway station: Penshurst (2 miles)
Parking:	In a lay-by on B2176 leading north of the village
Refreshments:	Pubs and tearooms in Penshurst and Chiddingstone

Penshurst and Chiddingstone are both real Kentish gems. Penshurst is set in a scoop of hills with the rivers Eden and Medway joining forces in the meadows below. Chiddingstone stands on a minor ridge overlooking the Eden Valley and out to the blue line of the greensand hills walling it to the north. Penshurst has its magnificent Place, a huge mansion set in extensive parkland; Chiddingstone has its Tudor street and castle. Both have fine churches. All around unfold scenes of great beauty.

This walk links the two by way of the low hills that edge the snaking River Eden as it works its route to the Medway. There are woods and undulating meadows, big views and bubbling streams and photogenic oast houses; an undemanding stroll amid fine scenery, with plenty of birdsong and colour in the hedgerows.

* * *

132

The outing begins at the northern (uphill) end of the lay-by on B2176 on the edge of Penshurst (1) opposite Penshurst Place. A farm drive cuts away left (west) to Salmans Farm. There is a sign for the Eden Valley Walk (2) near the start of the drive, and you follow these waymarks for much of the way towards Chiddingstone.

Wandering down this tree-lined drive you soon cross the River Eden. Just beyond it the drive forks. Take the right-hand track which slopes uphill, and soon gain a view down onto the River Eden. At the top of the rise Chiddingstone church tower may be seen half-right ahead, and a pair of oast houses that will be passed later on the walk. Far off, the greensand hills merely hint at their charm. Near at hand wild flowers line the track while birds flit to and fro, chattering.

The track leads to the farmyard of Wat Stock (GR: 506438). To the left, partially screened by farm buildings, the old half-timbered farmhouse, ageing on the ground like something from Henry Fielding or Thomas Hardy, seems not to belong to the modern world. Walk straight ahead, soon to pass more houses. The track curves and you come to a large pond on the right. Just after this there's a stile on the right beside a field gate. Go over the stile and cut across the field beyond, making towards the left-hand edge of a deep wooded hollow where another stile leads out to a narrow country road.

Bear right for a few yards, then go left onto a track (sometimes quite muddy) that runs alongside conifer woods. Before long the track slopes down to cross a little brook, and about 50 yards beyond it you leave the Eden Valley Walk and follow a footpath which breaks away half-right, sloping gently uphill.

Come to a stile and a junction of paths. Continue ahead, pass a small pond on the left, then bear half-right across the crown of the hill. Notice the tower of Chiddingstone church rising out of the hollow ahead, and the shape of Chiddingstone Castle to the left, half-hidden by trees. *(I once came this way in late spring on an early Sunday evening, the air filled with the fragrance of the season, the evening light soft and spreading shadows, and as the church tower rose out of that hidden landscape ahead, so the bells began to ring for Evensong. It was a touch of man's magic to mingle with that of nature all around me. A moment to savour.)* Another stile is crossed and the path edges alongside a sports field, between fences, and eventually brings you to the street of Chiddingstone village (3).

Note: To visit Chiddingstone proper, and this is after all one of the purposes of the walk, turn left here and wander a few yards along the road. Houses, inn, teashop, Post Office Stores and church are all clustered together. But if you plan to visit the castle you must continue along the road beyond the church.

Resuming the walk, turn right along the road and follow it to a junction of lanes at Larkins Farm (GR: 506453). Standing in an 'island' at the lane junction is a clutch of converted oast houses, while there are more off to the right, in a meadow. It's a charming scene, with a backdrop of folding hills and meadows and patches of woodland.

Take the right fork and continue down the road. At the foot of the slope you come to the hamlet of Wellers Town. The road crosses a stream and immediately after you'll see a field gate on the left with a stile beside it. Cross the stile and wander along the left-hand edge of the field until you come to a gateway by a large oak tree. Go through the gateway and continue along the left-hand boundary of a large field. Halfway along you'll see a hop garden off to the left.

On the far side of the field come to a metal gate and a stile. A few yards after having crossed the stile bear left over a little brook, then half-right towards an arched footbridge that will take you over the River Eden. Having crossed the Eden turn right, pass the end of a woodland, then bear left up the slope with the wood on your left and a pair of dutch barns seen on the skyline ahead. At the top of the slope pause for a moment to enjoy the panorama spread before you.

The way continues beyond the dutch barns, goes alongside the garden boundary of a house on the right, then descends a flight of steps onto the B2176 road. The parkland of Penshurst Place is opposite. Turn right and walk down the road, with care, into Penshurst.

Items of interest:

1: Penshurst. Even without the massive stately home of Penshurst Place, the village would still be worth visiting. Its setting is full of charm. Its cluster of timber buildings that hang over and around the original Leicester Square (named after the first Earl of Leicester) are

The original Leicester Square at Penshurst

most attractive. The sandstone church itself, 800 years old but with much reconstruction, holds plenty of interest, and with impressive memorials to the Sidneys of Penshurst Place next door, while the old forge along the street, with its great horseshoe door, must be reckoned the most attractive garage in Kent.

It is, though, to Penshurst Place that the majority of visitors go. This vast building, standing like Knole in a great sweep of parkland, was begun in about 1340 by a wealthy wool merchant, Sir John de Pulteney, who was Lord Mayor of London no less than four times. In 1430 it was bought by the brother of Henry V who added to it. But it is the Sidney family that has cared longest for Penshurst Place, for they came in 1552 and have been here ever since. During their time queens, princes and poets have danced in de Pulteney's Great Hall and walked through the gardens. Ten acres of garden are contained by walls, of which the poet sang: "The blushing apricot and wooly peach/Hang on thy walls, that every child may reach..." It is one of Britain's finest stately homes, a great pile of mellow stone and timber halls containing history, romance and treasures of another age. The house and its gardens are open to the public at set times.

135

2: Eden Valley Walk. Promoted by Kent County Council, the Eden Valley Walk links Edenbridge and Tonbridge by 14 miles of footpath, bridleway and country lane. As its name suggests, it explores some of the best features of the Eden Valley, and finishes with a riverside walk from near Penshurst to Tonbridge by the side of the Medway. Guidebook: *Eden Valley Walk* by Caroline Wing is published by KCC. The route is also described in the companion to the present guide: *Walking in Kent Vol II.*

3: Chiddingstone. Details of this fine village will be found at the end of Walk 23.

WALK 25: PENSHURST - LEIGH - PENSHURST

Distance:	4½ miles
Maps:	O.S. Pathfinder 1228 'Tonbridge & Edenbridge' 1:25,000
	O.S. Landranger 188 'Maidstone & The Weald of Kent' 1:50,000
Start:	Penshurst (GR: 527438)
Access:	Via B2176 about 4½ miles south-west of Tonbridge. Nearest railway station: Penshurst (2 miles)
Parking:	In a lay-by on B2176 leading north of the village
Refreshments:	Pubs and tearoom in Penshurst

This is another popular walk that provides broad vistas of a lush green countryside. For lovers of trees it is especially rewarding, for although there are no woodlands as such to wander through, there are avenues of stately plane trees, enormous ancient oaks, clusters of limes and beeches, seemingly as old as time. A great number were destroyed by the '87 storm, but there are still plenty left to enjoy. Part of the walk follows the Medway in a secluded corner; a walk that may be followed at any time of the year, although after prolonged rain the meadows down by the river could be under water. Each season has its own particular charm.

*   *   *

In the main street of Penshurst (1) the Leicester Arms almost faces onto the charming little courtyard of Leicester Square; a much photographed scene of steps and tiles and heavy-beamed cottages overhanging the entrance to the churchyard. Just below Leicester Square, at a bend in the road, an archway leads into the grounds of Penshurst Place, with a footpath sign indicating the way to Killick's Bank and Ensfield.

Go through the archway and along the drive beyond (part of the Eden Valley Walk), with the high wall of Penshurst Place on your left. The drive soon becomes a farm road that makes a slight curve to the right, with sparse woods and a pond on the left, then begins to rise towards Well Place Farm, seen ahead. Shortly after the pond cross a stile on the left, turn right along the field boundary and come to a second stile. Over this walk up the slope half-left to a marker

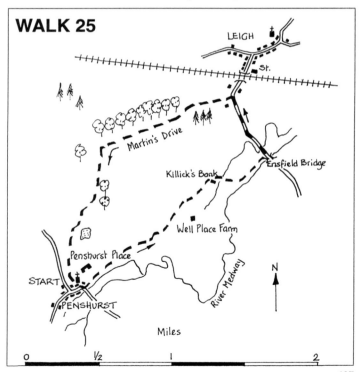

post on the crown of the hill. At the top spare a few moments to gaze behind at a fine view, with the spires of Penshurst church seen peeping over the trees, and the turrets of Penshurst Place giving a hint of grandeur.

Continue in the same direction to an avenue of trees running from Well Place Farm. Ahead there is a field gate and a stile giving access to a large hilltop field. The way leads along the right-hand edge of the field, and shortly after comes onto a concrete farm road. There are wide views ahead, with Tonbridge seen in the valley, and tree-lined hills far away.

The concrete road eventually slopes down to a group of cottages at Killick's Bank, passes to the left of these, then forks. Take the right branch for a few yards, then strike away downhill towards the bottom of the slope. Marker posts lead the way. At the foot of the slope cross a sturdy footbridge, beyond which flows the Medway - here a broad river in low-lying meadows. Bear half-left to it, then walk along the left bank until you come to Ensfield Bridge (GR: 547453). Go up onto the road and bear left for about half a mile.

Arrive at the top of a hill with the entrance to Pauls Hill House on the left, and a track running alongside it.

Note: If you plan to visit Leigh, or are in need of refreshment, remain on the road, now going downhill, pass beneath a railway bridge and continue to the Fleur de Lis pub in the village.

The circular walk continues by turning up the track and wandering through a screen of trees to reach a field. Keep along the right-hand boundary and into a second field beyond. Off to the right are views of the greensand hills; an enchanting vision of wooded hills and patchwork meadows dotted here and there with farmhouses. Come to a pond on the edge of the field. Just beyond this the path veers slightly to the left and brings you to the start of a long avenue of plane trees, known as Martin's Drive. Wander along this avenue. On either side there are woods or spinneys. Now and then they break away to show the hillside plunging into a little coomb; there are blue-hinted views to right and left - especially fine to the left where a soft light filters through the trees and brings with it the gift of space. Rabbits and hares race along the evenue's leaf-strewn carpet, and birds sing you through with a fanfare of song.

The avenue leads on for about half a mile. Midway along it go through a V-gap squeeze stile next to a field gate, and continue ahead to the far end of the evenue. One path breaks off to the right, the way ahead is private, but the left-hand grass path entices downhill, soon along another avenue of trees, and with the lake of Penshurst Place seen ahead slightly to the right.

Shortly before reaching the bottom of the slope, keep a lookout for an ancient oak off to your right, fenced around and with a large field behind it. This is known as Bear's Oak, for reputedly the last bear in England was killed beside it. Some 20 yards or so beyond it cross a stile in the fence, turn left and wander alongside the fence boundary, soon with a close view of the lake with its ducks and geese and bulrushes. The way continues across the parkland of Penshurst Place, passing to the right of a cricket pitch and leading by way of stiles (conventional and squeeze-type) towards the great mansion. Go alongside the low right-hand boundary walls and hedges of Penshurst Place, and into the churchyard. Walk through this and beneath the arched buildings of Leicester Square into the heart of the village.

Items of interest:

1: Penshurst. Details of both village and stately home are given under Walk 24.

WALK 26: PENSHURST - FORDCOMBE - PENSHURST

Distance:	7 miles
Maps:	O.S. Pathfinder 1228 'Tonbridge & Edenbridge' 1:25,000
	O.S. Landranger 188 'Maidstone & The Weald of Kent' 1:50,000
Start:	Penshurst (GR: 527438)
Access:	Via B2176 about 4½ miles south-west of Tonbridge. Nearest railway station: Penshurst (2 miles)
Parking:	In a lay-by on B2176 leading north of the village
Refreshments:	Pubs and tearoom in Penshurst, pub in Fordcombe

On this walk we explore the upper valley of the Medway, a peaceful valley held between gentle curving ridges upon which there are some fine houses, and from which there are memorable views. Fordcombe, which marks the turning point on the circuit, sits close to the Sussex border. Without being exactly picturesque, it's nonetheless a cheery place with some delightful countryside spreading away from its crossroads. An altogether pleasing community with a village green, pub, general stores and a string of trim, typically Kentish houses.

For this latest edition of Walking in Kent the route has been altered slightly and improved. Now there are even better views to enjoy.

*   *   *

From the lay-by on B2176 walk along the road into the heart of Penshurst (1). Turn left at the T junction and continue along the road, passing Leicester Square and the archway entrance to Penshurst Place, and go downhill to cross the Medway. Beyond the river the road begins to climb, and immediately after passing a house on the right named Holly Bank, turn right on a track that enters fields.

The track curves leftwards, narrows to a footpath and goes along the top edge of two fields, with the extensive grounds of Swaylands - a stone-built mansion used today as a boarding school - spreading away to the left. On reaching the end of the second of these fields cross a stile in the corner and continue ahead with an interesting view of a timber-framed house in the dip before you. This is Old Swaylands, and beyond it the broad cut of the Medway's valley stretches between converging hills. Come to a track that leads to a driveway. Turn right and walk past the entrance to Old Swaylands, gaining a privileged view of this splendid old manor (GR: 534426).

Pass a black converted barn and follow the drive until it forks. Go straight ahead to a stile on the left, opposite a house. Over this wander through a small field to a gate, and continue ahead through a gap in a hedge, over a stile and half-right across two adjacent fields linked by more stiles. In the third field bear half-left to find yet another stile in the boundary hedge. This leads into a hop garden. Turn right along its edge and soon reach a stream, a tributary of the Medway. Turn left and, finding a footbridge, cross the stream and wander over a meadow to reach the Medway by a bridge (GR: 533421).

Follow the river upstream (the Medway to your right); pass through a squeeze stile and continue ahead. On reaching a second squeeze stile you'll find a plank footbridge on its far side crossing a deep cut with a watercourse flowing through it. Over this bear left and walk up the field away from the river, keeping a line of trees on your left. At the top of the field an enclosed track leads up to a narrow country road beside some houses. Turn right to pass Hamsell Farm (GR: 535415).

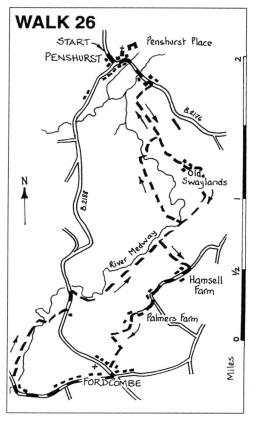

WALK 26

Walk along the road for half a mile. It bends sharply to the left by some cottages, then forks soon after. Take the right fork - a drive leading to Palmers Farm. Go through the farmyard, but on coming to some tile-hung cottages on the right of the drive, turn left, cross some metal bars in the hedge and then bear half-right up a sloping field. Pass through a gap by a holly tree in the upper boundary, continue up the left-hand edge of the next field, then turn right along its top edge. In the right-hand corner of this field find a stile on the left - but note

141

the beautiful far-reaching views back towards the north.

Over the stile ignore another on the right, and continue up the edge of the field towards its top corner. Before reaching this cross some bars (or a stile) on the right into the corner of a hilltop field, with Fordcombe church seen on the far side. Wander through the middle of the field to its far corner where there's a gate and a stile beneath an oak tree near some houses. (More magnificent views to enjoy behind.) Now go ahead between gardens to reach the B2188. Turn left and in a few yards come to the crossroads in Fordcombe (2) (GR: 527403).

Turn right down Chafford Lane which goes alongside a cricket ground, passes a site for mobile homes, then a row of cottages, and brings you to the Medway (3), here seen as a pleasant winding stream snaking through low meadows. (Those who know the Medway at Rochester may find it difficult to relate this as the same river!) Leave Chafford Lane beyond the road bridge by crossing a stile on the right, and amble beside the Medway through the meadows. You'll pass a flood barrier which hastens the river's flow, but it soon becomes less frenetic and conjures a peaceful atmosphere.

On reaching a footbridge cross to the right bank, then bear left to the road (B2188) shortly after. Go along the road towards a hump-backed bridge. Do not cross the bridge but instead go over a stile on the right immediately before it, and follow the Medway round the headland of several fields for about a mile. Eventually the river bank brings you to the plank footbridge over the deep cut of a watercourse crossed on the outward route. Continue alongside the river, but on coming to the substantial bridge crossing the Medway (GR: 533421), bear left and go over it to the left bank.

Walk ahead on a clear path to the far side of the first field where the way forks. Bear right, then go half-left through a gap and across the next field. The path maintains direction and eventually rejoins the Medway at a footbridge. Cross to the opposite bank and bear left round a field edge. When the boundary veers right, go with it, soon to reach a crossing path. Turn left, now on the homeward stretch which leads to the familiar track heading back to Penshurst.

Items of interest:

1: Penshurst. Details of both village and stately home are given under Walk 24.

2: Fordcombe. Its position above the Medway, with Sussex hills mingling with those of Kent nearby, makes for a charming corner of countryside. Good walks to be had locally; the Wealdway passes through, and the Sussex Border Path makes a by-pass round it. None of its houses is old (they're all of either the 19th or 20th century; and the church dates only from 1847), yet the gathering round the green makes a pleasing picture, and there's something most agreeable about the whole village.

3: The Medway. Kent's major river begins life in Sussex and enters Kent between Groombridge and Ashurst where it marks the county boundary. Later, it cuts right through Kent to its estuary beyond Rochester. The river is tidal as far inland as Allington, near Maidstone, and is navigable from its estuary to Tonbridge. Between Tonbridge and Rochester the river is accompanied almost continuously by a towpath that provides delightful walking. See Walk 28 for the 16-mile stretch from Tonbridge to Maidstone.

WALK 27: TONBRIDGE - ASHURST

Distance:	12 miles
Maps:	O.S. Pathfinder 1228 'Tonbridge & Edenbridge' and 1248 'Royal Tunbridge Wells & Forest Row' 1:25,000
	O.S. Landranger 188 'Maidstone & The Weald of Kent' 1:50,000
Start:	Tonbridge Castle (GR: 589465)
Access:	The castle is on the left bank of the Medway in Tonbridge High Street. Nearest railway station: Tonbridge
Parking:	Various public car parks in Tonbridge
Return travel:	Train from Ashurst (not Sundays) to Edenbridge Town, then 1 mile walk to Edenbridge Station for the Tonbridge line
Refreshments:	Pubs, cafés and shops in Tonbridge. Pubs en route at Haysden, Bidborough, Modest Corner, Speldhurst, Fordcombe and Ashurst

The Wealdway is a long-distance walking route that begins in Gravesend on the banks of the Thames, and finishes 82 miles later on the clifftop of Beachy Head. On its way it discovers some of the best and most varied scenery in the south-east. One of the early stages is that which links the historic town of Tonbridge (the largest on the Wealdway after Gravesend) with the sunny village of Fordcombe, set near the border with East Sussex. It begins with a 2-mile stroll along the banks of the Medway, then proceeds with a series of sloping fields and woodlands up to the panoramic ridge-top village of Bidborough. It then continues to explore the high country of Wealden hills, where meadows and sudden valleys and dappled woods conspire to create one delightful landscape after another. Speldhurst retains an attractive heart; an interesting church, a fine old inn, and broad canvasses spread in all directions. Fordcombe gives a taste of Sussex. Below it winds the young Medway (see Walk 26), and beyond that the meadows of another county.

In order to allow a practical return to Tonbridge by train, it's necessary to continue beyond Fordcombe to reach Ashurst Station. But the additional 2½ mile walk from Fordcombe to Ashurst is well worth tackling for itself. It's a charming stretch of countryside and one that makes a worthy finish to the walk.

Note: With the privatisation of British Rail there is a question-mark hanging over the future of the Uckfield-Ashurst-Edenbridge Town line, so check the availability of trains before setting out.

*   *   *

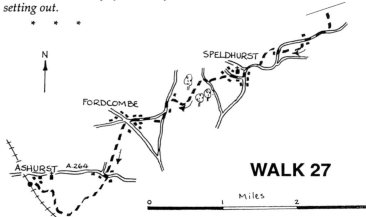

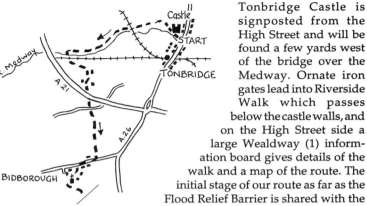

Tonbridge Castle is signposted from the High Street and will be found a few yards west of the bridge over the Medway. Ornate iron gates lead into Riverside Walk which passes below the castle walls, and on the High Street side a large Wealdway (1) inform-ation board gives details of the walk and a map of the route. The initial stage of our route as far as the Flood Relief Barrier is shared with the Eden Valley Walk.

Turning your back on Tonbridge (2) go through the gates and walk ahead along the tarmac path that has the river on one side and the castle walls on the other. Leading among trees and flower beds, it is most attractive. The way then crosses a side stream, passes a model railway and goes over a narrow road to follow a minor stream that flows beside you on the right. Continue straight ahead and walk along the edge of a large parkland meadow, then pass beneath a low railway bridge. The path crosses the side stream again, wanders through a wooded area and bears left to cross two more streams before regaining the bank of the Medway proper. The way now goes ahead along the northern bank of the river and comes to an iron footbridge known as Lucifer Bridge (GR: 576465).

Do not cross this but continue along the footpath. No longer surfaced it soon leads alongside meadows or fields and shortly before reaching the big grey gates of the Flood Relief Barrier, you should cross the river by a concrete footbridge. Bear right, then soon veer left to pass the Heusenstann Friendship Wood and go under another low railway bridge. Ignore a bridge on the left, go through a gate and straight ahead over a footbridge, bear left immediately on meeting another path. Then veer right to cross two more footbridges and come to a broad track that leads to the hamlet of Haysden. Pass to the right in front of The Royal Oak and go down the rough lane beyond. At the end of this turn left to reach a farmyard. Here bear right, go through a gate into a field near a converted oast house, and cross to the far left-hand corner. There you will find a foot tunnel beneath the A21 Tonbridge bypass (GR: 570452).

Emerging from the tunnel turn left, go over a footbridge and immediately turn right. Follow the boundary hedge to reach a stile giving onto a country road. Cross to a gap opposite, and walk up the sloping field to a small wood. The way continues along its right-hand edge, passes through a gateway to the left-hand side and, still walking uphill, goes through the wood to the B2176 road at Bidborough (3). Turn right and a few yards later note the panorama out to the right. The Medway lies some distance below, but beyond it the Greensand Ridge forms a long barrier, while to the north-east lies orchard country with the North Downs beyond that. A big countryside, green and fertile and most attractive.

Continue along the road for about 500 yards. On the left-hand side a footpath sign directs the way to the church. The path leads through a small residential area, past a sports field and up a slope into the churchyard. There you will find another glorious sight, with the ancient church overlooking cottage rooftops and more fine views, this time out to the west.

Pass in front of the church, go down the path and out through the lych gate. Bear left by the village school and wander down Spring Lane. When the lane curves left, go straight ahead on a footpath among trees, then over a stile to reach the foot of the slope. Here you cross a small footbridge and walk up the opposite side with a fence to your right. Find a stile by a large oak tree and cross over to go through a woodland. On emerging from this cross another stile into an open field where you bear half-right and make for the left-hand corner of a cemetery fence. Go down the slope ahead and in the valley bottom cross a footbridge near a spinney, go over a stile and up the slope, then veer right. The path leads directly to Modest Corner (GR: 572423).

Turn right to pass in front of a row of cottages, in the midst of which stands The Beehive pub. Continue down the slope beyond, cross a cemetery access road and come onto a winding country lane. Turn right and walk along it for about half a mile. On the left, opposite a driveway leading to The Birchetts, will be found a metal swing gate with a footpath sign. Go through this and walk across two fields, keeping a hedgerow on your left. At the far boundary of the second field, turn right and walk along the headland to a stile. Continue in the same direction over two more fields, then down a slope to another stile giving onto some steps that lead down to a road.

Bear right for a short distance, but immediately beyond a white house (Forge House) turn left across its drive and onto a footpath leading to a stile, beyond which you go down a steep hillside to a stream. An access road takes you ahead now to pass a former mill, whose pond is seen to the left. On coming to a road turn right and follow it to a junction whose left fork takes you into Speldhurst (4).

Pass the 14th-century George and Dragon Inn, and take the right fork where the road divides by the church. About 200 yards along this road go through a metal swing gate on the left, where a footpath sign directs the way to Bullingstone Lane. The footpath leads behind some houses and into a large field with broad views to the right. Cross the field ahead, then down through a sloping woodland to Bullingstone (GR: 545412). There are some lovely old cottages along this lane, set in a peaceful corner. Turn right, and about 80 yards later go left between a pair of 15th-century cottages. At the entrance to Avery's Wood the path forks. Take the right-hand option which descends to a stream. Cross by footbridge and up the slope beyond; an enchanting patch of woodland. Follow the path through the wood until it brings you out to a meadow fenced for paddocks. Walk diagonally across this making for the far left-hand corner.

Come to a country road and turn left. Wander along it towards a converted oast house opposite another road signposted to Fordcombe. Ignore this and continue ahead to reach another road junction, this time to the left. On the right a Wealdway marker directs the path through a gate and up some steps. Passing one or two buildings go straight ahead into a field and pass a tennis court to your left. A stile leads onto another road where you turn left and walk along it for a little under half a mile to a crossroads at the village of Fordcombe (5) (GR: 526403).

Cross to the playing field opposite, and walk across it to the far left-hand corner. The path continues ahead along the edge of several fields with fine views to the right. Going through the last field towards Stone Cross Farm, come onto a driveway near converted oast houses, veer right and reach the A264 East Grinstead to Tunbridge Wells road.

Cross the road with care, turn left and, when it curves sharply to the left a few paces later, go down an enclosed footpath on the right. This takes you alongside paddocks before another enclosed footpath section leads to a charming meadowland, with conifer woods on the left. Walk ahead through the meadowland towards an enticing view of distant hills with woodlands on their crown and chequered fields on their slopes.

Keeping left of the ridge wander ahead to a stile by a field gate with a cattle trough nearby. Over this walk on towards a sloping line of trees. There are two field gates with stiles beside them. Cross the left-hand stile and walk down the slope beyond, following the right-hand hedgerow. Halfway down the slope cross a stile on the right into the next field, then continue down the slope to pass through a small woodland. Out of this bear right (on the route of the Sussex Border Path) and wander alongside the wood. Come to a gateway near some farm buildings and continue ahead, now on a track that soon curves to the right. Keep along the track until another breaks away to the left. Now walk down a slope between hedges to Jessup's Farm. Bear right in front of the farm and follow the driveway to Ashurst Station.

Note: For those in need of refreshment, continue along the station road to find The Bald-Faced Stag pub on the main road. Note also that the station here is unmanned, so tickets need to be bought from the train's conductor.

Items of interest:

1: The Wealdway. A long-distance route of 82 miles that links Gravesend on the Thames with Beachy Head on the Sussex coast. Scenically varied, it explores some of the most attractive countryside in southern England. Guidebook: *The Wealdway & The Vanguard Way* by Kev Reynolds (Cicerone Press).

2: Tonbridge. There was a hillfort here in Iron Age times; its name is thought to have come from the old English *dun burgh* which means hill fort. But it is the remains of the old Norman castle, standing above the river, that distinguishes the town today.The original castle was built to defend an important river crossing on one of the few north-south trackways through the Weald. This was shortly after the Norman Conquest, but it was almost completely destroyed by fire in 1087. A replacement was built almost immediately, which is an indication of the site's strategic importance.

Elsewhere the town has several fine old buildings, including the 16th-century Chequers Inn not far from the castle, and another timber building of the same period next door. Up the hill a short distance away stands Tonbridge School; all mellow stone and neat lawns, founded in 1553 as a Free Grammar School, but almost completely rebuilt in Victorian Gothic style in 1864.

3: Bidborough. A charming hilltop perch with views overlooking the north, east and west. The church of St Lawrence is a small sandstone place of worship with a glorious panorama from its doors. It has stood firmly bedded on the ridge since the Normans were here. Within it holds the peace of all those ages, and it is only the heavy swinging of the clock's pendulum that breaks the silence of a thousand years. Dark and crowded among the pews, it is nonetheless one of the gems of this walk.

4: Speldhurst. Another delightful hill village, this one with Saxon links. Mentioned in a document of A.D. 768, it overlooks country that lies on the fringe of the Wealden iron-making region. Indeed, just outside the village to the north-west, Barden Furnace Farm occupies the site of one of the smelting works of by-gone times. The church is a sturdy Victorian replacement of an earlier Norman structure badly damaged by lightning. In it there's some stained glass by William Morris and Burne-Jones.

5: Fordcombe. Details of this village are given under Walk 26.

WALK 28: TONBRIDGE - MAIDSTONE

Distance:	16 miles
Maps:	O.S. Pathfinder 1228 'Tonbridge & Edenbridge', 1229 'Paddock Wood & Staplehurst' and 1209 'Maidstone' 1:25,000

	O.S. Landranger 188 'Maidstone & The Weald of Kent' 1:50,000
Start:	The Castle pub, Tonbridge High Street (GR: 591465)
Access:	The Castle is situated near the bridge over the Medway. Nearest railway station: Tonbridge
Parking:	Various public car parks in Tonbridge
Return travel:	Train from Maidstone West to Tonbridge via Paddock Wood. (Intermediate stations at Beltring, Yalding, Wateringbury and East Farleigh.)
Refreshments:	Pubs, cafés and shops in Tonbridge and Maidstone. Pubs at several strategic points along the way

This non-circular walk is the longest in the book, but there are several places en route where, if desirable, it can be cut short with a train back to either Tonbridge or Maidstone. It's a pleasant stroll, practically level walking from start to finish along the Medway towpath for most of the way. It's scenic, peaceful, colourful, and it ventures into the very heart of Kent. There are no real route-finding difficulties. There are locks to cross, weirs to wander by, medieval ragstone bridges spanning the river which sometimes winds between orchards, sometimes through meadowlands. Sometimes it's tree-lined and shady; never is it dull or uninteresting.

The Medway is navigable from Tonbridge to the sea, and along it there will undoubtedly be river craft slowly chugging, or negotiating the many locks that control the water's level and flow. Canoeists and anglers find their own sport; sometimes there will be oarsmen training. Mostly, though, there will be only birds and animals and insects for company. And a broad, ever-changing horizon.

At opposite ends of the walk both Tonbridge and Maidstone are historic towns that repay a visit. But it is the river that holds the true value of this outing. The river and the countryside through which it threads a course.

* * *

An attractive bridge takes Tonbridge High Street over the Medway near the castle ruins. The Castle pub stands on the south side of the bridge , with Medway Wharf Road cutting alongside it. Turn down this road and shortly after join the towpath on the riverside, and walk ahead, soon to reach the first of many locks. Continue below a gasworks and on to a road serving a small industrial estate on the

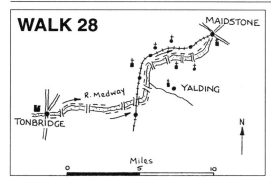

outskirts of Tonbridge (1). Now cross to the left bank of the river and wander ahead, almost immediately stepping into countryside. Two more locks are passed before the Medway Navigation path ducks beneath Hartlake Bridge (2) (GR: 629473).

Along this stretch of the river Hadlow tower (3) is clearly seen across the fields; sometimes directly ahead, sometimes to one side as the river winds its way along. A little under a mile beyond Hartlake Bridge you come to East Lock where it is necessary to cross to the right bank once more. For almost 3 miles now the river leads through a deserted, peaceful countryside - the most remote of the whole walk. Woods and meadows remain in view, and distant hop gardens and orchards. South of East Peckham the path goes through trees on a small island accessed by footbridges, passes another lock and a sluice and shortly after comes to a small industrial estate by a road at Branbridges.

Cross the road to a works entrance, and rejoin the riverside path, still on the right bank. Not long after this go beneath a railway bridge. The river is shaded by trees for a while, and grows more attractive as you approach Yalding, with orchards lining the hillslopes ahead. The river grows busy at The Lees where the first of the medieval bridges (Twyford Bridge) is met. There's a weir, more lock gates, a large pub and refreshments at a café beside the river near a boat chandler's.

The navigable river turns to the north here. Cross by the lock and head north too, along the B2162 road. On reaching a bridge taking the road over the river, bear right on a marked footpath which runs along the left bank beside a factory wall. The next stretch, as far as Nettlestead, is often rather overgrown with giant hogweed towering

Square-walled oasts on the Medway near Yalding

beside you in summer. The path passes below Nettlestead church
(4), which is worth a short diversion to see. (The church is a simple,
cool place of whispers and solitude. A footpath crosses the railway
line and leads up to it, providing a sly glance of medieval Nettlestead
Place next door.)

The towpath remains on the left bank all the way to Maidstone,
although there's a pleasant alternative stretch on the right bank
from Bow Bridge at Wateringbury to Teston Lock. At Wateringbury
the riverside is like a mini seaside resort; at Teston there's a lock and
a weir, with the remains of an old mill on the right bank, and a fine
ragstone bridge. (Public toilets in the car park left of the river near
the bridge.) At East Barming a wooden bridge spans the river,
followed by another very pleasant stretch that leads to the
connoisseur's bridge of East Farleigh. Farleigh Bridge has several
arches striding through the river, and a fine lock just beyond. All
around there's much to see and to admire, with the view up to the
village dominated by its church and a cluster of oast houses.

On reaching Maidstone (5) the riverside has been tamed by

concrete. But on the opposite bank there's an old church, a college and the former Archbishop's Palace guarding the Medway; mellow buildings, ducks in the river and, a short way ahead, the full bustle of the county town.

To reach Maidstone West Station walk ahead to the stone bridge, go onto the road and bear left. The station will be found about half a mile away up the hill.

Items of interest:

1: Tonbridge. Details are given under Walk 27.

2: Hartlake Bridge. The present bridge replaces a somewhat frail timber structure that was the site of a tragedy in 1853. On their return to camp from a day spent harvesting, 35 hop pickers from London, riding in two waggons, broke through the bridge rail and were tipped into the river below. All 35 drowned: men, women and children. They have a memorial in Hadlow church.

3: Hadlow tower. Clearly seen across the fields on this walk, the tower is also known as Hadlow Castle, or May's Folly, for it was built at the end of the 18th century by Walter Barton May, a wealthy and eccentric industrialist. The castle to which it was attached no longer stands, but the tower remains as a dominant landmark 170 feet high. See also Walk 16.

4: Nettlestead church. A small 15th-century building of weathered stone stands above the river and next door to the medieval manor of Nettlestead Place. Much of the original stained glass in the church was destroyed by a hailstorm on 19 August 1763 when 10-inch diameter hailstones smashed the windows and wrought havoc in neighbouring villages.

5: Maidstone. The county town of Kent is a mixture of old and new. In places there's a successful blend of styles and ages, in others a glaring architectural horror story. The best belongs to the past. Down by the river the former Archbishop's Palace rises almost from the water. Originally used as a manor for the Archbishops of Canterbury, it passed out of the hands of the church in 1537 when Cranmer exchanged it with Henry VIII for other properties. Today it is rented out for private functions. In dungeons beneath the palace John Ball was once imprisoned for preaching social revolution.

Nearby stands the ragstone church of All Saints, considered by many to be the grandest Perpendicular church in Kent. There are many other fine buildings too: the Master's House of the College of Priests, a lovely old gatehouse, and the former Archbishop's Stables housing a carriage museum.

WALK 29: COWDEN - FURNACE POND - COWDEN

Distance:	3 miles
Maps:	O.S. Pathfinder 1228 'Tonbridge & Edenbridge' and 1248 'Royal Tunbridge Wells & Forest Row' 1:25,000
	O.S. Landranger 187 'Dorking, Reigate & Crawley' and 188 'Maidstone & The Weald of Kent' 1:50,000
Start:	Cowden church (GR: 466405)
Access:	Via signposted road south-west of B2026 about 3½ miles south of Edenbridge. Nearest railway station: Cowden (1¼ miles)
Parking:	With discretion in Cowden High Street
Refreshments:	Pub in Cowden

In a leaf-shrouded valley tucked away from the world there runs a narrow lane beside a boggy region of shoulder-high bulrushes, of willow and alder, swamps of wild garlic and bluebells. There's an outcrop of rock with beech trees hanging over. And there's a long pond whose ripples alone disturb the stillness. It is an enchanting place, yet once it rang to the hammers of the ironmasters. The pond, this great stretch of peace and harmony that holds jealous guard to a no-man's-land of tranquillity, was once a furnace pond in a time when the might of England's industry looked to Wealden iron for its war machines, as to its gates of splendour. Once the valley sounded to the hiss of steam and the clanging of iron. Today birds warble in the foliage of overhanging trees.

A glance at the map will show Cowden's position amid this one-time industry. There's a Furnace Farm and this furnace pond, Hammerwood and two farms with Cansiron in their titles. Wandering the lanes and trackways we find that several are deeply sunken - cut by the wheels of heavily laden waggons carting ironstone for centuries through the hills and valleys to be worked at the furnaces. No doubt a number of the fine houses scattered nearby were the homes of former ironmasters. History hangs in the air.

Cowden has been largely saved from the excesses of our somewhat graceless age. Its street is lined with white weatherboarded houses and tile-hung cottages. Its church is shingled from tower to spire and all around lie peaceful acres of green. Kent Water, the stream that separates Kent from Sussex, winds just a field or two away. Surrey edges meadows and woodlands a short stroll to the west. Cowden seems, somehow, to have taken some of the best from each, and it cares for them well. This walk gives a brief taste of what it has to offer.

*   *   *

Facing the church of St Mary Magdalene in Cowden High Street (1) turn right and walk towards the centre of the village, then take the first road on the right and follow it as it twists its way out of the village, soon to have fields and trees on either side. On coming to a sharp right-hand bend you will see the gateway entrance to Waystrode Manor directly ahead. Go through the gateway and walk ahead down the drive, passing on the right an attractive pond. Towards the end of the drive, where it suddenly swings left, there is another pond - also on the right. To the left can be seen the impressive timber-framed manor, which is more than 500 years old. Leave the drive at this bend and walk ahead to enter a woodland through the right-hand of two wooden gates.

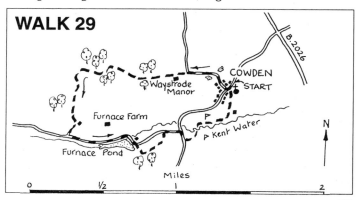

A footpath takes you through the woods. About two-thirds of the way through it forks. Take the left fork here and shortly after cross a footbridge over a deeply cut stream and come out of the woods. Walk directly ahead across an open field and go through a gap into the next field, which is almost completely encircled by trees. Continue to the far right-hand corner where you will find another gap leading into Clay's Wood. There is a track which forks a few yards later. Bear left and soon come to a large clearing.

Turn right and walk round the boundary to pass an old barn almost hidden by trees and bushes to your right. Just beyond this go through yet another gap where there is a field gate and a stile. Over the stile walk up the left-hand side of the next field. Near the top bear left over a stile and wander half-left across the corner of another field to pass through a gap. Bear half-left again to the bottom right-hand corner to find another stile set beside a field gate. Turn right and follow the woodland shaw all the way until you come to a sloping field with a house standing off to your left. Go over a stile and bear half-left to the right-hand side of the house, then through two wooden gates onto a sunken lane. Bear right and walk down to a T junction. Take the left-hand lane and note a few yards later an attractive outcrop to your left, with trees growing over it (GR: 448400).

This lane is followed for about half a mile, and is interesting all the way. At first there are trees on either side, and in springtime the ground beneath them is amassed with wild flowers. Then to the right comes a boggy section with more wild flowers and marsh-loving plants and insect life. Then comes the long furnace pond, bordered by trees and with reeds growing in the shallows at its edge. At its north-eastern end a stream pours out of the pond down a series of steps beneath the lane and down to a hinted wonderland below to the left. Here the lane makes a sharp right-hand bend and trespasses into Sussex. A few yards later it swings leftwards. At this left-hand bend leave the lane and go straight ahead into woods on a clear track which forks a few paces later. Take the left-hand option which soon slopes uphill.

Among birch trees and bracken you come onto Holtye Common and follow the path which skirts its left-hand edge. On reaching a junction of paths bear left, soon descending among trees to the lane once more. Turn right and follow the lane a short distance to a T junction by a weatherboarded cottage named Kitford Mead (GR: 460400).

Turn right on the road signposted to Holtye, and shortly after passing a house named Framptons, leave the road to find a metal swing gate on the left, next to a field gate among chestnut trees. Through the gate walk straight ahead to a stile, cross it and enter a new golf course. Go down to the stream, which you cross by the second footbridge, thus returning into Kent. Bear right and follow the stream for about 250 yards to reach a hedge boundary of a house. Bear left and walk uphill on a footpath alongside this boundary. Cross a driveway and enter an allotment area where the footpath leads directly to Cowden church.

Items of interest:

1: Cowden. A lovely village saved from being overrun by traffic by the fact that no main road passes through. Its street is lined with half-timbered houses, weatherboarded or tile-hung cottages, a one-time inn opposite the church, and the former village school with a Tudor air - alas no longer will local children be taught here. The church of St Mary Magdalene has marked this gathering of three counties for 600 years; the shingles of its spire overtop the trees that rise in opposition all around. Waystrode Manor is quite 500 years old, for it was mentioned in a will of 1471. It is but one of many ancient dwellings that grace the village and its neighbouring acres.

WALK 30: COWDEN - HOATH CORNER - COWDEN

Distance:	8¹/₂ miles
Maps:	O.S. Pathfinder 1228 'Tonbridge & Edenbridge' 1:25,000
	O.S. Landranger 188 'Maidstone & The Weald of Kent' 1:50,000
Start:	Cowden church (GR: 466405)
Access:	By signposted road south-west of B2026 about 3¹/₂ miles south of Edenbridge. Nearest railway station: Cowden (1¹/₄ miles)

Parking:	With discretion in Cowden High Street
Refreshments:	Pubs in Cowden and Hoath Corner

This is one of my favourite walks in the book. Interest never wanes. The scenery is seldom short of delightful, and there are surprises waiting round every corner. It begins by following the Sussex Border Path eastwards along the banks of Kent Water - the stream that marks the boundary between Kent and East Sussex - through countryside green and gentle, before climbing over Hobbs Hill. This provides a memorable panorama that encompasses a broad canvas stretching from east to west; it's all highly picturesque. Now heading northward we skirt Stonewall Park and drop into a bowl of light trapped by encircling hills and woodlands, where vineyards cover acres of secluded farmland.

From vineyards and woodlands a footpath climbs onto another hill with a view, and in the corner of a field there's an outcrop of sandstone under which badgers have scraped their setts. During research for the first edition of this guide I discovered a huge beech tree astride a gap between two large rocks, allowing the unique experience of being able to stand directly beneath the upright trunk of a still-growing tree! Alas, that fell victim to the '87 storm like so many others.

Hoath Corner is reached by a lavish bluebell wood, and in the tiny hamlet the thirsty wanderer will be pleased to find refreshment before continuing along a lane, through more fields and woods to an isolated farm, and soon after another rocky outcrop, higher and broader than the first, and to a climber a challenging sight. From there a series of fields leads back to Cowden.

In springtime an abundance of bluebells and wild garlic along stream-bank and hedgerow, as well as in the woods, becomes an overpowering sight, and matched against the blossom of wild cherry, crab apple and blackthorn, and the multi-shades of green leaves, makes for a highly colourful and fragrant outing. Add to that many different habitats to divert the attention of the amateur naturalist, and it's likely that the walk will take far longer to complete than the actual mileage might otherwise warrant. And why not?

*   *   *

Walk through Cowden (1) churchyard, passing the church to your left, and leave by way of a gate in the bottom corner to find a footpath leading down the edge of a field, with a brick wall on your

WALK 30

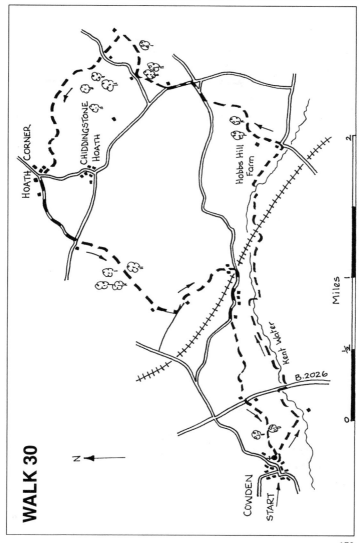

N ←

HOATH CORNER

CHIDDINGSTONE HOATH

Hobbs Hill Farm

Kent Water

B.2026

Miles

2   1   ½   0

COWDEN

START

right. Beyond the wall the path continues straight ahead enclosed by fences, and comes to Kent Water opposite the attractive Sussex House Farm. Go through two or three field gates and continue ahead on the left bank of the stream through two fields, the second of which has a stile leading directly onto the B2062 road (GR: 474404).

Turn right, cross the road bridge and enter East Sussex. A few yards beyond the bridge cross a stile on the left into the corner of a field. Now walk ahead along the edge of the field for about 250 yards until you come to a footbridge that will take you back into Kent across the stream. Turn right and follow the stream through more fields. Before long you pass below a large collection of farm buildings (Moat Farm), and here you cross once more to the right bank of Kent Water. Ignore a second bridge over the stream and continue along the right bank.

Kent Water disappears beneath the bramble-covered embankment of the Edenbridge Town to Uckfield railway line. (If there have been no trains running, you'll barely guess that the railway passes here.) Continue along the edge of more fields, over one or two stiles, until suddenly you arrive at a brick archway that has been disguised until the last moment. The path goes through the archway and out to another field. Bear half-right to rejoin the stream. Soon you come to a footbridge, this one with a gate to it. Ignore it and continue for a further 50 yards or so until you reach another footbridge, which you cross.

Turn right, once more wandering along the left bank through yet more fields, until you come to a very narrow road a little below a house, and with Hobbs Hill Farm seen with its oast house halfway up the hill to the left. Bear left along the road, and straight up the hill towards the farm. The farm drive swings left by the oast house, and here you leave it and continue ahead through a gate and up a sunken track among pine, oak and beech trees; a delightful gully of a track, overhung by trees whose gnarled roots claw for a hold on the steep banks. At the top, where the angle eases, pause for a moment to enjoy the views seen through a gateway, or between the trees (GR: 503408).

The footpath veers to the right along the edge of the hill with more views to enjoy off to the right through the trees, then it swings leftwards among trees and bushes, and is soon enclosed over the brow of the hill, with fields on either side. Eventually come to a country road (GR: 505413). Turn right, and at a crossroads shortly after, turn left. Keep along the road for about 200 yards then, a few paces after passing a house on the right, find a stile leading into a field. One path follows the right-hand hedge, but we aim diagonally across the field to the far corner where it is bordered by woodland. Come to another stile half-hidden by a hazel clump. Stonewall Park can be seen off to the left.

Do not go onto the road here, but bear half-right along another footpath cutting across a field to the left-hand end of a woodland. A few yards from the woods go through a gap into the next field and walk straight ahead towards a large house seen on the far side. On reaching its boundary fence turn left, pass alongside a group of trees hiding a pond, and continue over the field to a pole carrying power lines among trees. Go down some steps and across a country road to a narrow path that plunges steeply down a slope beside Courtlands Wood.

Walking down this path there are superb views to the Greensand Ridge in the distance, but nearer to hand, in mid-view, a collection of vineyards (2). Halfway down the slope cross a stile in the fence and go across a field bay, walk through a projecting line of trees and continue down the slope to a footbridge. Over this continue across the next field to the far corner and a pair of footbridges at right-angles to one another. These lead to the edge of a woodland, with a vineyard on the right.

Bear left round the woodland edge, then over another footbridge and half-right through a spinney. Near the head of the slope, after about 200 yards, bear left along a track. (Ignore a footpath on the right which goes to Penshurst.)

Out of the trees cross a stile seen to the left of a field gate, and go straight ahead along the right-hand edge of a field. Continue in the same direction up a slope towards a red tile-hung cottage. Find a stile a little to the left of the cottage leading into a 'tunnel' of trees and hedges. Come to a track and walk along it as far as a lovely timber-framed house. Opposite, on the right, go up a few steps, over a stile and ahead along the left-hand edge of a field with large views to the right. At the end of the hedgerow bear left and walk up the next field beside a wooden fence. At the top of the field the way forks near an outcrop of rocks.

A track leads ahead, but we bear right round the edge of the field to a stile in the fence. Over this enter woods and follow the path as it winds through. When it forks take the left-hand option. Come out of the woods to an open meadow, bear right and walk through it towards a house on the far side. Here come to a road at Hoath Corner (GR: 497431). Turn right, and a few paces later come to a junction of country roads, with The Rock pub nearby. Turn left and walk along the road for $^1/2$ mile towards Mark Beech. Come to another road junction and bear right, then almost immediately turn left through a gate next to the drive of a house, and walk ahead along a track.

At the end of the track go through a gate on the right and wander half-left across the field to a woodland. Locate a stile next to a small wooden gate and walk ahead on an enclosed path along the left-hand edge of the woods. Overgrown in places, it eventually comes to a junction of paths where you bear right and descend a slope to a footbridge over a stream. The path climbs on the far side and emerges to a large field. Walk ahead along its left-hand edge, and when the trees finish continue straight ahead up the slope to a stile in a hedgerow gap. Over this aim to the left of a pair of cottages and come onto a driveway. Follow this to the left, through a gate and down to a narrow lane. Turn left and follow the lane to its end at Wickens Farm (GR: 483415).

Continue beyond the farm for a few yards along a track towards yet more woods, but reaching the edge of these wander along an enclosed footpath leading off to the right down the side of the woods. When you come to a stile cross over and bear half-left across a slope to a gateway. (Note the sandstone outcrop on the left as you cross the slope.) A track leads beyond the gateway, then bears right downhill to pass through a farmyard at Sandfields Farm, and onto a country road.

Go ahead along the road, over a railway bridge and follow round for about 600 yards. On the way pass a farm and a group of houses on the left. Then, a little beyond these, Moat Cottages. The road bears right, and here you cross a stile on the left into a narrow field. Across this go over a second stile into a large open field. Walk ahead along its left headland and pass a footbridge at the bottom. The boundary curves to the right, and 150 yards later you'll see a second footbridge on the left with handrails. Across this bridge walk straight ahead over another field, passing a pond and a woodland on the left. Enter a final field, bear half-right and walk across it to join the B2026 road just to the left of a house (GR: 473407).

Cross this road with care to an enclosed footpath with a little woodland on its left. This leads to a large field which you cross half-left to find a stile on the far side, in an angle formed by the junction of two lines of trees. A series of stone steps now leads down through a little woodland to a footbridge spanning a stream. Go up the opposite slope and out by way of yet another stile. Cross to the corner of a scrubby woodland shaw, walk through it then descend to the left to a final footbridge. The slope beyond leads directly to Cowden churchyard.

Items of interest:

1: Cowden. Details of this attractive village are given under Walk 29.

2: Penshurst vineyards. Although the Romans introduced the grape to Kent, and in the Middle Ages monks cultivated vines in various parts of the county, the art of viticulture practically died out for several centuries. In recent times, however, Kent has seen a marked development of vine growing, and vineyards are becoming very much a feature of Wealden landscapes. At Penshurst the vineyards are open to the public by appointment with the owners, and Penshurst wines are on sale locally.

The High Weald

Snug in its hollow Tunbridge Wells is something like the body of a spider. Stretching out in all directions are its legs - the ridges of the High Weald. Hills push into Sussex to the south and south-west among outcrops of sandstone, among green woodland bowers and up to the great open heath of Ashdown Forest. To the west runs a whale-back ridge that forms a southern boundary to the valley of the infant Medway. On it squat villages like Fordcombe and Ashurst, visited elsewhere within these pages on walks setting out from points along the river.

To the east of Tunbridge Wells, and to the south-east, High Wealden hills are lush, green, benevolent. Their slopes are either smooth with parkland meadows and lit by banks of rhododendron and azalea, or strung about with hops, lined with orchards or neat linking vineyards. Prosperous villages, whose original wealth came from the iron and wool trades of the 15th and 16th centuries, look out upon a landscape of artistic husbandry. Brenchley is rich in half-timbered houses that belong to another era; Goudhurst occupies the summit of a hill that gazes out, it seems, over all of southern England, historic, charming, bustling; Lamberhurst with its sweeping hills, its vineyards, its magnificent lakeside ruin set amid a riotous garden of colour, and its memory of the iron industry.

One-third in Kent, two-thirds in Sussex, Bewl Bridge Reservoir is England's largest inland water south of the Thames. Oast houses and heavy-beamed farmhouses look out across its meadow-lined bays, and footpaths trace a route around its shores. A short step east of this the great expanse of Bedgebury Forest rolls across the Weald; but a part of this forest fills us with wonder, for there's nothing quite like it anywhere else in these isles. Bedgebury Pinetum boasts Europe's finest collection of conifers - 200 species of them. Set out on gentle hillsides sloping into tight little valleys and coombs, there are magnificent redwoods and cypresses, silver spruce and juniper and Scots pine and Chilean pine and many, many more. There's a lake set among shrubs and trees that flows out of the Pinetum and into another, much larger, lake in the grounds of Bedgebury Park, home of the Bedgeburys in the Middle Ages, then of the Culpepers, but now housing a boarding school.

The Culpepers were everywhere in the Weald, and in Goudhurst's lovely hilltop church they are there by the dozen. There are Culpepers in brass, in stone and in wood. One collection forms a group of eighteen, eleven of them kneeling. Another family numbers a dozen. One lies at rest with her hair carefully braided, another reclines still in his armour. Old Sir Alexander had an iron foundry at Bedgebury that cast the guns that fought the Spanish Armada, and in other corners of this fertile agricultural land, there are reminders of Kent's past dependence upon iron.

Between Brenchley and Horsmonden, surrounded now by trees and hops, there stretches a large furnace pond that, like Cowden's, once drove the hammers that pounded iron into shape. And at Lamberhurst the railings that went round St Paul's Cathedral were made.

Lamberhurst is visited today, not for its iron, but for its gardens. Scotney Castle, one of the National Trust's many spectacular properties, dreams in a hollow by a lake. Full of romance is this grey ruin, with its circular tower, its medieval stone bridge and its flush of foliage. Built in 1379 by Roger de Ashburnham, most of what we see today belongs to the 17th century, but in the late 1830s Edward Hussey aided its 'picturesque decay' with delightful eccentricity. He quarried stone for a new house and filled the quarry with exotic shrubs and trees and flowers, creating a garden that is one of the treasures of the High Weald.

The walker here may never run short of ideas. There are footpaths tracing from hilltop to hilltop, running through orchards and among the hops, into woods and across open parkland.

It's a colourful region with subtle light playing. In early autumn there's a muskiness in the air as the harvest of hops takes place, and of an evening working oasts have a glow of non-stop activity about them. Orchards come into their own in May, and throughout summer there's a heavy thrum of insect busyness in the grasses and among the trees. Yet winter is not devoid of charm either, and a skyline of leafless chestnut, oak or beech can be as thrilling to the countryman as are the blossoms of spring.

*   *   *

WALK 31: BRENCHLEY - HORSMONDEN - BRENCHLEY

Distance:	6 miles
Maps:	O.S. Pathfinder 1229 'Paddock Wood & Staplehurst' and 1249 'Wadhurst, Cranbrook & Bewl Bridge Reservoir' 1:25,000
	O.S. Landranger 188 'Maidstone & The Weald of Kent' 1:50,000
Start:	Brenchley church (GR: 680417)
Access:	Via minor road branching east of B2160 at Matfield. Brenchley is on Tunbridge Wells-Tenterden bus route
Parking:	Public car park opposite the Post Office, near the church
Refreshments:	Pub and shop in Brenchley; pub $\frac{1}{2}$ mile from end of walk

Today the High Weald is a garden of blossom; a fertile land of orchards, hop gardens, vineyards and meadows flecked with grazing sheep. A peaceful scene; a harmony of colour and soft sounds; the rich benevolence of nature laid out for inspection. But once it was a veritable power-house of industry as Britain's iron was pounded into shape. Where now songbirds fill the silence of Kent's green acres, once there sounded the crash of hammers, the roar of steam and the air was filled not with bright buds but sparks. As at Cowden (Walk 29) there may still be found the tell-tale signs of this past industry, and on this walk we stumble upon a great stretch of water that was a furnace pond when this surprising land lay at the heart of England's 'black country'.

We also wander through numerous orchards, past grand country houses and into parkland that contains two more lakes in as calm a setting for a picnic as one could wish.

Brenchley, where our outing begins, is an attractive village of Tudor cottages in an almost perfect street - black beams and white plaster, an oast house, handsome sandstone church and a triangle of grass supporting a single tree. Wat Tyler is said to have lived in a cottage at the top of the hill, and more recently Siegfried Sassoon grew up here and committed the surrounding countryside to literature in The Weald of Youth. From the village the huge outlying landscapes beckon with a promise readily fulfilled.

* * *

At the southern end of the pretty street in Brenchley (1) a half-timbered shop faces the triangle of grass with the parish church nearby set back behind its avenue of yew trees. An enclosed footpath goes down the left-hand side of the shop, but where it makes a sharp left turn, another goes ahead, over a stile and into a sloping field. Wander down the slope to a woodland corner, then up the other side. When the woodland ends orchards stretch away to the right. Continue ahead and eventually come to a narrow lane beside a pair of bungalows at Palmer's Green, and turn right.

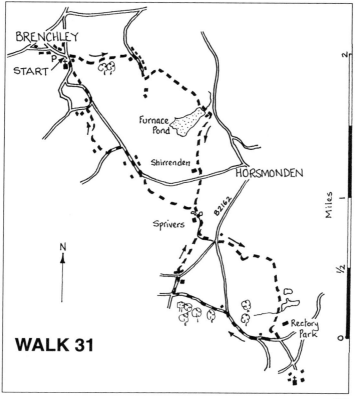

WALK 31

Passing a typical Kentish tile-hung cottage on your left, the lane (now a farm drive) enters orchard country with Hononton Farm seen ahead almost completely surrounded by row upon row of fruit trees.

Halfway down the drive turn left and walk along a broad track dividing two sections of orchard. On coming to a crossing line of trees acting as a wind-break, go through them and turn right along another track leading to hop gardens. Continue ahead between two hop gardens, with Horsmonden seen in the distance. Come to another farm drive, cross it and follow the left-hand boundary of the next hop garden, and so reach the corner of a large furnace pond. The footpath traces the pond's left-hand edge - a delightful place with fish jumping, birds singing, and the rush of the stream flowing from it through trees and down a series of steps (GR: 695413).

At the end of the pond walk ahead for a few paces, then bear right to pass along the left-hand side of Lake Cottage. Continue on a grassy track between a conifer plantation on one side and orchards on the other, and come to a large meadowland with the stately house named Shirrenden seen at the far end. Wander over the meadow to find a stile and a field gate well to the left of the house. Beyond the stile continue ahead and come to a country road opposite the entrance to Sprivers (2), a country house whose gardens are open to the public through the auspices of the National Trust.

Walk down the drive towards Sprivers, passing duck ponds, then the house itself, and continue to the end of the drive which brings you out near a junction of country roads at Hazel Street. Cross slightly left to find a footpath leading into an orchard. Walk through this and continue in the same direction through a hop garden. When this ends turn right for about 50 yards, then go left across an open field, through a line of pollarded trees and into more orchards. Maintain direction along the left-hand edge of a line of trees dividing orchards, cross a track and bear half-right. A gap in the boundary hedge leads to another junction of roads in front of a house (GR: 702395).

Turn right, cross a stile beside a beech hedge that runs alongside the house garden, and walk down the left-hand boundary of a large meadow. At the end go over a stile beneath an oak tree, and on to another stile giving access to Rectory Park. Wander across this, with two lakes seen to the left fed by a stream in a tight cleft below. There are some lovely mature trees scattered about the parkland, and the massive 18th-century Old Rectory seen at the top of the opposite slope. Cross the feeder stream by a wooden footbridge, then up the hillside beyond, keeping well to the right of the Old Rectory, and come to a narrow lane (GR: 702386). Ahead stretches a broad panorama, with the hilltop village of Goudhurst on the horizon; a peaceful, gentle view.

Note: Directly ahead a lane runs for about ¹/₂ mile to Horsmonden church, set among oast houses. A church without a village nearby.

On leaving Rectory Park turn right along the lane, and in 400 yards come to a junction of country roads. Continue ahead. At the next junction (GR: 696389) bear left and walk on for about a third of a mile between Coalbank Wood on the left and orchards on the right. Come to a minor crossroads and turn right for a further 250 yards to yet another road junction with a few houses standing on the north side. Leave the road here and walk ahead on a track between houses to enter an orchard. Walk through the orchard, pass through a gap in the far hedgerow and come to an iron gate leading on to the familiar drive which goes to Sprivers. Bear left, and when you reach the duck ponds go sharp left and follow the track as it leads beside a wood, then hazel coppices, and eventually reaches the Brenchley-Horsmonden road.

Bear left for about ¹/₂ mile, with views of orchard-clad hillsides and Brenchley church beckoning ahead. The road slopes downhill. Near the foot of the slope turn left into Spout Lane. In about 150 yards the lane veers leftwards, but we go to the right on a track. Pass to the right of a bungalow and follow a fence to a stream. Cross into the field ahead, and bear half-right to a stile in a wooden fence. Continue in the same direction to another stile by a field gate. Over this walk along a track beside a pond, and come to a narrow lane. Turn right along it to the Brenchley road near The Halfway House pub (GR: 683414).

Turn left and wander along the road as it winds up towards Brenchley. About 200 yards or so beyond the pub a footpath marker directs you to the right, up a flight of steps and into a sloping field. Brenchley church is seen directly ahead. Cross the field, over another stile and down onto the road. Brenchley High Street is a few paces away to the right.

Items of interest:

1: Brenchley. This is one of the most handsome of High Weald villages, with a charming street of timber-framed, tile-hung or weatherboarded cottages and houses. The heart of the village is tiny and grouped around a triangle of grass in front of the church. The sandstone church is some 600 years old and approached along a pathway between clipped yews. The rood screen, dating from 1536, is a fine example of the craftsmanship of a bygone age.

2: Sprivers. Originally a timber-framed house that was encased in brick in the mid-18th century. It has large gardens of shrubs, herbaceous borders, old walls and spring and summer bedding. The gardens are open to the public by the National Trust on set days between April and September.

WALK 32: LAMBERHURST - KILNDOWN - LAMBERHURST

Distance:	4 miles
Maps:	O.S. Pathfinder 1249 'Wadhurst, Cranbrook & Bewl Bridge Reservoir' 1:25,000
	O.S. Landranger 188 'Maidstone & The Weald of Kent' 1:50,000
Start:	Lamberhurst High Street (GR: 676363)
Access:	By A21 about 7½ miles south of Tunbridge Wells
Parking:	Public car park behind The Chequers pub in the High Street
Refreshments:	Pubs and shops in Lamberhurst; pub in Kilndown

Lamberhurst's countryside is among the finest in all Kent. Spread in every direction are landscapes of appealing beauty. Hills fold neatly into little valleys to create individual scenes begging to be converted onto an artist's canvas. Streams snake through these valleys to impose their own character - none more so than the Teise - and to drain a rich and well husbanded region of orchards, hop gardens and vineyards.

There are handsome houses too. Lamberhurst has its fair share of them, as witnessed by a stroll through its streets. An attractive village that sadly suffers the indignity of summer traffic trundling nose-to-tail along the

A21 that cuts through its very heart. (A by-pass has been long promised. Whenever it comes it'll be a mixed blessing. On the one hand it will save the village. On the other it'll destroy some fine countryside.) Lamberhurst has its old coaching inns, weatherboarded shops and cottages lining the streets, and a one-time industry that contrasts the aura of serenity that comes from its neighbouring acres. The iron industry is all but forgotten, replaced by England's largest vineyard as a centre of attraction, and by the glory of nearby Scotney Castle.

Scotney is reached along a rhododendron-flanked drive leading from the main road. Owned and maintained by the National Trust, the castle ruins reflect in its beautiful lake, with towering gardens of shrubs and trees, and surrounded by a graceful cropped parkland. This walk cuts through the parkland, and passes within yards of the castle entrance. Given time (and time should be allowed for it) you are urged to visit the castle and its gardens for an unforgettable vision of loveliness.

* * *

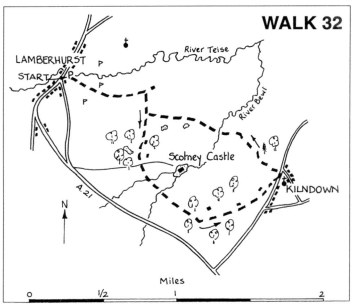

From the car park at the rear of The Chequers, walk directly through the playing field to a stile on the far side, giving access to Lamberhurst golf course. The way leads across a fairway, through and alongside a hedge, by the side of a tee and over a stile to a narrow field. Cross this to a clear track rising uphill to a group of pine trees, from where a lovely view left shows Lamberhurst church (1) a couple of fields away. At the gateway entrance to a house, turn right over a stile and walk up the left-hand edge of a sloping field.

On the far side of the field cross another stile and about 50 yards later go through a squeeze stile on the left, then maintain direction among large parkland trees, soon going down a slope aiming to the right of a lone cottage seen on the edge of woodland. Cross another stile well to the right of the cottage, go over a driveway and follow a clear path through the woods. This brings you to the main drive leading to Scotney Castle (2) (GR: 685354).

Note: To visit the castle and its gardens, bear left along the drive.

Continuing the walk, cross the drive and go through a metal gate into a delightful rolling parkland. Go down the slope half-left to a little bridge over a stream. This is the Sweet Bourne which flows through Scotney's lake and joins the River Bewl (the second stream we cross shortly) on the other side. The Bewl then boosts the Teise at Finchcocks Bridge, and after gathering more waters from the Weald, finally spills into the Medway near Yalding.

Cross the bridge and follow the track to a second bridge. On the way you may just see Scotney Castle ruins largely screened by trees off to the left. The track rises gently uphill towards woodland, and goes into them through a gate at the head of the slope. After about 200 yards come to a junction of tracks and bear left on a route signposted to Kilndown. Wandering along this track there are several others breaking from it, but yellow waymarks provide guidance. After a while pass just to the right of an isolated house. Soon after, the path goes alongside a line of stately beech trees. Emerging from the woods wander past a row of cottages and eventually come to a road on the edge of Kilndown (3) opposite The Globe and Rainbow Inn (GR: 701353).

Turn left and almost immediately go left again where a footpath sign indicates the route back to Lamberhurst. A clear and obvious track takes you ahead through Kilndown Wood. As you begin to go down a slope views open ahead. Come to an area of pines and bear right on another track that winds downhill. This track leads all the way through the woods and eventually brings you to a stile and a field gate leading to more parkland. A footbridge is seen about 100 yards ahead across the narrow River Bewl. Over this the way continues up the slope along the right-hand edge of a meadow.

At the top of the meadow come onto an estate drive and bear left. About 100 yards later cross a stile on the right with a sign directing the way to Lamberhurst again. Wander over the crown of the hill making for the far right-hand corner of the hilltop meadow. There you rejoin the outward route. Follow the footpath back to the group of Scots pine trees, descend left down the track and over the golf course back to Lamberhurst village.

Items of interest:

1: Lamberhurst church. Dedicated to St Mary, this fine church, in a glorious setting, was built in the 14th century. It has a Perpendicular tower with a shingle spire rising from it. Inside there's a triple-decker pulpit of 1630, with very fine carvings. The original deck, on which the parish clerk sat, has now gone.

2: Scotney Castle. A mellow turret, last of the original four, stands two-dimensional in the lake. Plants claw their way up the stone blocks and trail in the water. Built during the Hundred Years War it was considerably rebuilt by the Darell family who lived there for three and a half centuries. In 1778 Edward Hussey bought it from them, and it was his grandson, another Edward, who made the gardens and, after building the mansion that today houses the National Trust's southern headquarters, encouraged the castle's 'decay', thus creating much of its present romance and beauty.

The great storm of 1987 felled a number of mature trees and badly damaged the gardens, but the dedication of National Trust staff and volunteers in the months that followed was rewarded, and visitors today would be hard-pressed to imagine the havoc wrought by those winds. Once more Scotney Castle gardens reflect the glory of nature and the genius of man.

3: Kilndown. It is the church at Kilndown that draws one's attention. Not ancient, as many of Kent's churches are ancient, nor is it lovely in the way that Lamberhurst's is lovely. But interesting, certainly. Built in 1840 by Viscount Beresford, it was originally a squat sandstone place without grace or pretension. But Alexander Beresford Hope, his stepson, set out to change all this, and transformed the church by hiding its box shape with a parapet round the tower from which great gargoyles stare down - truly Gothic. Inside are highly coloured carvings - a Crucifixion on the reredos, the font and its cover, the chancel screen - and vivid colours in the windows, made by craftsmen from Munich under Franz Eggert.

WALK 33: LAMBERHURST - GOUDHURST - LAMBERHURST

Distance:	8 miles
Maps:	O.S. Pathfinder 1249 'Wadhurst, Cranbrook & Bewl Bridge Reservoir' 1:25,000
	O.S. Landranger 188 'Maidstone & The Weald of Kent' 1:50,000
Start:	Lamberhurst High Street (GR: 676363)
Access:	By A21 about 7½ miles south of Tunbridge Wells
Parking:	Public car park behind The Chequers pub in the High Street
Refreshments:	Pubs and shops in Lamberhurst; pubs, shops and tearoom in Goudhurst

Hop gardens and orchards feature heavily on this outing, for our paths lead either alongside or through many of each. It will therefore be apparent that blossom time makes this a very special walk, and later, at the tail end of summer when the hops are being harvested, there will be a weighty fragrance in the air, and the fields a mass of industry.

The walk leads through the valley of the Teise, both on the outward and the homeward journeys. Here, the little river flows peacefully through its cut, bordered by the wild extravagance of nature under harness. From the vantage point of neighbouring hills this valley of the Teise is a gentle expression of summer indolence. It encourages a slowing of pace, invites the walker to pause for a while and become contemplative. No bad thing in country such as this.

WALK 33

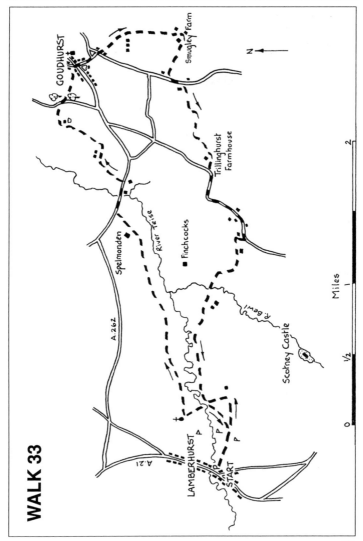

GOUDHURST

Smugley Farm

N

Trillinghurst Farmhouse

River Teise

Spelmonden

A.262

Finchcocks

R. Bewl

Scotney Castle

Miles

LAMBERHURST

A.21

START

0   ½   1   2

Goudhurst marks the turning point. This hilltop village has its glory sung both far and wide, which is understandable. A most attractive winding village, it is typical in its Kentish architecture of many different periods, and with huge commanding views. The purpose of this walk is to explore that landscape for a full flavour of its own special atmosphere

*   *   *

Leave the car park at the rear of The Chequers and walk across the playing field to the far side where a stile leads onto Lamberhurst golf course. Cross a fairway, then go through a gap in the hedge and ahead with a hedge on your right. Continue past a tee and over a stile to a narrow field. Cross this and walk up a clear track rising towards a group of Scots pine trees where there's a crossing path. Bear left and descend through a large field to a footbridge crossing the River Teise, and go up the next field towards Lamberhurst church (1).

Do not enter the churchyard, but turn right and recross the field towards a hop garden. Come to a footbridge over a ditch with a farm bridge beside it. Cross into the hop garden and walk ahead along a concrete farm road. After a while it makes a sharp right turn. Leave the road here and continue ahead, still in a hop garden. On reaching the far side go through a gate and into the field beyond where you maintain direction. Off to your right will be seen the cluster of oast houses at Little Scotney Farm (the homeward route passes just below them), and ahead to the right, the large baroque house known as Finchcocks (2). The River Teise twists its way round the right-hand boundary of the field. Ahead there are more oast houses and a large number of buildings at Spelmonden Farm. Beyond rises the cone of a hill with Goudhurst spread across its flanks.

On the far side of the field go through a white gate by a ditch, and bear right along the boundary of the next field. At the far right-hand corner cross a stile and continue in the same direction. Come to a field corner, bear right for a few yards, then go over another stile and continue on the left headland of the field beyond, with farm buildings up the slope to your left. Maintain direction through a gateway and across a field to pass between Spelmonden Farm on the left and a long low brick building on the right. Now join a concrete farm road between hop gardens and out to the A262 (GR: 706373).

Turn right and walk along this road for a short distance. Crossing the Teise again note the watermill on your right, Hope Mill, with oast houses behind it. On coming to the Green Cross Inn (there used to be a railway crossing here) go over to the left-hand side of the road to a footpath heading north away from the road. After about 150 yards cross a stile on the right among cypress trees, then turn left to resume direction along the edge of a field. At the far side enter the next field and maintain direction, but on the far boundary bear right and walk up the slope beside the left-hand hedge, on whose far side are one or two houses.

At the top of the field cross a stile, bear half-left over a farm drive and along a track with a hedge on your right, aiming towards farm buildings seen a couple of fields ahead. Along this track there are lovely views to be had, with hop gardens and oast houses and Horsmonden church some way off, with tree-topped hills and a great expanse of well tended countryside all around. It's a heart-warming agricultural scene, the land having been put to such good use over the centuries; husbandry at its best.

The track leads to the farmyard at Crowbourne Farm. Wander through to find a little pond on your right. The track divides in front of the red tile-hung house. Bear left on the drive which winds round the garden boundary, becomes a country lane, passes one or two houses, then reaches a T junction. Take the right fork for a few paces, then head to the left on a path leading into a steeply sloping woodland. At the top of the wood leave by way of a stile and continue up a long sloping field to its top right-hand corner where the continuing path goes between a high wall and a garden fence. Before taking this, however, pause for a moment to enjoy the broad vistas spread behind you. Far to the north on a clear day you can make out the Greensand Ridge above Yalding. The enclosed footpath leads directly out to the village war memorial and crossroads at Goudhurst (3). Opposite is an attractive duck pond (GR: 722377).

Note: For refreshments bear left into the main street where there are shops, tearooms and pubs.

To continue with the walk cross the main road, pass the duck pond to your right, and go down the B2079 towards Bedgebury (public toilets a few yards down the road). A short way down the slope the road makes a sharp right-hand bend by Whites Cottage.

Leave it here and walk ahead down a drive between houses. After some distance the drive makes a right-hand bend towards some timber-framed houses. At this bend go ahead on a footpath between a woodland shaw and fenced paddocks. At the end of the paddocks the path forks. Continue ahead on the right-hand option. Ahead, a couple of fields away, can be seen buildings belonging to Smugley Farm. Our route leads to them.

At Smugley Farm follow the track as it curves to the right round the buildings. Pass some converted oast houses and bear right again to walk along a farm road for about a third of a mile, following the route of a disused railway. On reaching a country road (GR: 721367) turn left and cross the stream which filters down to the Teise, and very soon draw level with the fine timbered Pattenden Farm seen to your right. Turn down the farm drive which leads past farm buildings and enters hop gardens.

After some time the track/drive forks. Stay on the main track as it curves leftwards and through a gate with some small buildings ahead. Now veer away to the right to find a stile leading over the right-hand fence into the adjacent hop garden. Continue ahead through this, cross a concrete bridge over a stream and follow up the right-hand side of the next hop garden. You will soon see oast houses off to the left.

At the end of the hop garden bear sharp left to continue along the boundary, but as you do, look back at the collection of oasts and more hop gardens making a patchwork countryside. On reaching a white gate go through it and walk across the meadow making for a point a little to the left of the converted oast houses (Trillinghurst Farmhouse) seen on the far side. There you join a farm drive and follow to its end.

The drive brings you to a country road (GR: 710362) where you bear left and wander along as it winds over the hills with lovely views to enjoy. There are some attractive houses spaced along the road for added interest. In a little over $1/2$ mile pass Hillside Cottage standing above the road on your right. Just beyond it a footpath sign directs the way onto the drive which doubles back to the cottage. Pass along its left-hand side and 50 yards beyond bear left up some steps and into a field near a barn. Walk ahead alongside the barn and below a grand-looking house seen up the slope to the left. Continue through this long field to its far right-hand corner where you cross a stile on the right, and immediately cross a second stile on the left. Then turn right again to a metal gate leading into Broadham Wood where a track leads clearly through.

Emerging from the woodland a peaceful scene greets you. Wander down the slope half-left, and through a gate onto a lane. Finchcocks stands a short distance down this lane, but we go left to cross a bridge, then cross a stile on the right just beyond it. Now cross a meadow to a stile on the far side, walking parallel with the right-hand hedge. Enter a second field, with Little Scotney Farm seen on the hill above, and wander across to the left-hand end of a hop garden which you enter through a gate. Walk along the left-hand edge of this hop garden, and leave it by a field gate on the far side into a flat meadow with the River Teise flowing along its right-hand boundary.

Bear left and cross this meadow to a field gate, and continue in the same direction, walking across a large field now in a line more or less with Lamberhurst church seen ahead. Eventually draw level with the river and reach the footbridge crossed on the outward route. Do not cross this, but continue straight ahead on a footpath which skirts the right-hand edge of the field to a second footbridge. This one crosses a ditch and leads into Lamberhurst golf course. Over the stile bear left for a few yards, then take the footpath across the golf course back to Lamberhurst village.

Items of interest:

1: Lamberhurst church. See notes accompanying Walk 32.

2: Finchcocks. An elegant red-brick baroque mansion built in 1725 for Edward Bathurst, today it is used as a 'living museum of music'. In it there are many historical musical instruments, and recitals are regularly held there. It is open to the public on set days.

3: Goudhurst. A much-loved village overlooking some of Kent's most productive orchard and hop-growing country, it has a busy main street lined with typical Kentish houses, shops and old inns. At the top end of the street stands the church with its solid, stumpy tower being a replacement of an earlier one burnt down in 1637. Inside this lovely place, which dates from the 13th century, is to be found a veritable art store of monuments to the powerful Culpeper family.

WALK 34: BEDGEBURY PINETUM - THREE CHIMNEYS - BEDGEBURY CROSS - BEDGEBURY

Distance:	4¹/₂ miles
Maps:	O.S. Pathfinder 1249 'Wadhurst, Cranbrook & Bewl Bridge Reservoir' 1:25,000
	O.S. Landranger 188 'Maidstone & The Weald of Kent' 1:50,000
Start:	Bedgebury Pinetum (GR: 714337)
Access:	Via B2079 about 3 miles south of Goudhurst
Parking:	Public car park at Bedgebury Pinetum. Note the time of closing
Refreshments:	None

The highlight of this walk comes right at the start with a ramble through the glorious rolling parkland of Bedgebury Pinetum, among 200-odd species of conifers set out by the Forestry Commission as Europe's largest collection of evergreens. It is a scientific collection, an open-air laboratory inspired after many of Kew Garden's conifers began to suffer the effects of pollution. Wandering the little hills and dells of this charming place one becomes enthused by the visual splendour of so many varieties growing in artistic landscapes. There are redwoods and cypresses and silver spruce, and rhododendrons too in bloom from late-winter to mid-summer. There are meandering streams, mirror lakes, lawn-like slopes, the colouring of shrubs and foliage, and birds darting to and fro.

The Pinetum is part of the larger Bedgebury Forest which covers some 2,500 acres of the Weald south of Goudhurst. Note that there is a fee to be paid for entry to the Pinetum - but it's worth every penny. Beyond it the walk explores the northern section of forest, then heads across farmland and alongside another lake with pleasing views.

*   *   *

From the Pinetum's large walled car park, go through a doorway in the wall corner and enter the Pinetum on a surfaced footpath. As you enter there are lovely views over sweeping lawn-like slopes adorned with graceful trees, tall, stately and elegant. With time to spare you are urged to wander round the grounds first before setting out on the walk proper, for there is much to see and to enjoy, and it would be a pity to miss the opportunity to explore this unique place.

Take the left-hand path which goes down the slope and eventually comes to Marshall's Lake. Pass round the right-hand end and join a broad crossing track. Bear right, follow signs to the public toilets, and leave the Pinetum through a gate behind the toilet building.

Turn right along a drive, and a few yards later go through a field gate to pass a Forestry Commission building on your left, and the Park House on the right. Bedgebury Forest stretches all around. Wander ahead on a broad track. After a while another major track joins ours from the right. Continue ahead, and soon the way curves leftwards and comes to a junction of tracks - almost a staggered crossroads. Maintain direction (the left-hand of two main tracks) and before long you reach a small group of cottages. Pass these to your left and continue on a track, then straight ahead at cross-tracks, still deep in the forest.

On reaching a T junction bear left and soon begin to emerge from the forest. Rising up a slope, the track curves to the right and at the top of the rise you break away left on a narrow, marked bridleway.

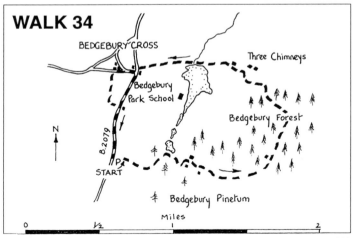

WALK 34

BEDGEBURY CROSS

Three Chimneys

Bedgebury
Park School

B.2079

Bedgebury Forest

N

P
START

Bedgebury Pinetum

Miles

0   ½   1   2

This takes you down a slope and about 70 yards later the bridleway forks. Take the right-hand trail which is enclosed by fences, and which brings you along a track to the left of a collection of converted oast houses, then onto a driveway. This is Three Chimneys (GR: 728347). Off to the left, in the valley, lies a lake with the chateau-like building of Bedgebury Park School (1) peering over the trees. Ahead, Goudhurst can be seen draped round its hilltop.

Shortly before reaching a solitary house, there is a pond on the left of the drive and two field gates. Go through the second of these into a large meadow and bear half-right across it. On reaching the brow of the meadow the lake can be seen again below. The path aims for the right-hand end, and there crosses the grass-covered causeway. Beyond the lake go ahead on a footpath leading up the left-hand side of another large field, eventually coming onto the B2079 road at Bedgebury Cross (GR: 717347).

Note: The most direct way back to the Pinetum car park is to turn left here and walk along the road for about ³/₄ mile.

Alternative route: Turn left and, a few yards later, take the narrow road heading off to the right. When it forks shortly after continue straight ahead to pass a row of cottages. Immediately after these bear left on a footpath into Combwell Wood. Go ahead through the wood, but should you stray from the vague path (easy to do), walk parallel with the road which is running some way off to your left. (If in doubt stray leftwards and you'll come to the road.)

When you meet a crossing path bear left and follow it to the road opposite an entrance to Bedgebury Forest. Turn right and walk along the road for about 500 yards to find the Pinetum car park.

Items of interest:

1: Bedgebury Park. The estate belonged to the Bedgebury family from the Middle Ages, but then passed into Culpeper hands through marriage. The house is a real curiosity. Originally a 17th-century brick construction, it was later encased in sandstone and considerably enlarged by Viscount Beresford (see note on Kilndown church - Walk 32). It was due to him that the huge house took on the chateau-like appearance we see today. It is now a boarding school.

WALK 35: FLIMWELL (PILLORY CORNER) - BEWL BRIDGE RESERVOIR - COMBWELL PRIORY - FLIMWELL

Distance:	5 miles
Maps:	O.S. Pathfinder 1249 'Wadhurst, Cranbrook & Bewl Bridge Reservoir' 1:25,000
	O.S. Landranger 188 'Maidstone & The Weald of Kent' 1:50,000
Start:	Pillory Corner near Flimwell (GR: 712322)
Access:	On A21 between Lamberhurst and Flimwell. Pillory Corner Picnic Site is opposite B2079 junction
Parking:	Pillory Corner Picnic Site
Refreshments:	Café midway along the walk

Created in the mid-seventies when the Southern Water Authority flooded several small valleys, Bewl Bridge Reservoir is the largest inland water south of the Thames. For much of its area it has retained a natural appearance with meadows, fields, orchards and woodlands sloping down its banks. It attracts waterfowl, of course, and on this walk a pair of binoculars could be handy - especially for the keen bird watcher.

The county boundary divides the waters unequally between Kent and East Sussex. Kent has the smaller area, but it is an attractive region with fine views along the reservoir and into Sussex. But the banks of Bewl Bridge occupy only one section of our walk. For the remainder, footpaths lead through woodlands and along the edge of several fields, and we gain a glimpse of a 12th-century priory set among comforting hills.

Pillory Corner Picnic Site, on a slip-road off the busy A21, has ample parking space, as well as a picnic area and public toilets.

*   *   *

Leave the car park and turn right to wander along the slip road towards Flimwell Farmhouse standing on the left. Just beyond it turn left and walk down a track which curves round the garden boundary, then swings right into a large field. Bear left round the field edge. It soon cuts away left and you continue with it for about 10 yards, then walk directly across the field making for a rather sparse line of trees leading down to woodland. Bewl Bridge Reservoir

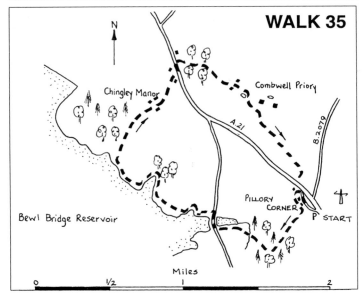

WALK 35

N

Chingley Manor

Combwell Priory

A.21

B.2079

Bewl Bridge Reservoir

PILLORY CORNER

P START

Miles

0   1/2   1   2

(1) is clearly seen filling the valley below.

At the foot of the slope use a wooden footbridge to cross a little stream (River Bewl) which here marks the Kent-Sussex border, and enter the woods. The path goes straight ahead up a slope. Just over the brow come to cross-tracks, turn right and follow the path downhill. *(It was here, one gusty morning in late winter, that I spent several minutes watching a goldcrest flitting among the branches of a nearby conifer. Unconcerned by my presence he preened himself barely inches from me, and gave a considerable lift to my day.)*

Ignoring side paths continue down to the foot of the slope where another stream is crossed into a small field. Aiming half-right across this come to a stile which gives access to an enclosed track leading to Rosemary Lane. Along the track keep an eye open for wildlife on the banks of a lagoon seen a few yards away to the right.

On reaching Rosemary Lane (GR: 700319) turn right and cross the causeway marking the eastern extremity of the reservoir. Just beyond this bear left on the driveway to Rosemary Farmhouse;

weatherboarded and tile-hung, it gazes out across the water. Immediately beyond the farmhouse go through a gate and follow the path ahead (the Sussex Border Path) with fine views of the reservoir. After about 300 yards you have a choice of routes.

Alternative path: This option cuts off a corner of the waterside path, but has the advantage of a slightly more elevated viewpoint. Cross a stile on the right and enter a field of fruit bushes where the footpath follows the right headland, providing a vista of reservoir, meadow and orchard, with neat low hills on the far side. At the end of the field cross another stile and bear right on the shoreline path.

Main path: Merely continue on the shoreline trail as it skirts the field, soon to be rejoined by the alternative path. The way continues, now heading north to go round a narrow inlet, then enters a coppice woodland. Out of this you go down the western side of the inlet, then after a while enter a larger area of woodland. This is Chingley Wood.

Almost immediately upon entering the woodland cross a stile on the right and go up the footpath beyond, signposted to Post Boy. It leads along the right-hand edge of a field through a gorse-lined sunken track, then through a woodland shaw (bluebells in spring). When you emerge from this continue ahead up the slope (fine views to the reservoir) to the brow of the hill and a junction of paths. Continue ahead, over a stile and along an enclosed footpath which brings you to the left of a converted oast house. Wander ahead now along a driveway, to pass the 16th-century Chingley Manor, seen to the left. Near the end of the drive you pass an attractive thatched cottage, and a few yards later come to the A21 (GR: 695337).

Cross the road with care, turn left and walk towards The Happy Eater café. Shortly before reaching this, however, turn right into Cats Wood (there is a footpath sign). Initially this is an untidy patch of woodland and the footpath may not always be clearly defined. But a few yards inside the wood you should see a trail. This leads slightly to the right among trees, and there are occasional markers to direct the way. The general direction is eastward, and the path trends a little to the right, then down to the edge of the woodland with a stream running alongside it.

Cross a plank footbridge, go ahead for a few yards, then bear left into the left-hand field. Follow the right-hand boundary, then continue ahead across the field to a stile and a gate leading into a large fence-enclosed field. Walk up the slope towards farm buildings, then passing through more gates and stiles pass to the left of them and down the slope beyond through another fence-enclosed field, this time parallel with a farm track on the left. At the foot of the slope the way now goes just to the left of a pond, and up the sloping meadow beyond aiming for a stile found to the right of more farm buildings.

The original footpath route took us close to Combwell Priory (2), but this has now been diverted and we only see the priory from a distance.

Over the stile enter a large parkland meadow and follow the left-hand fence ahead. This brings you round to a double field gate, beyond which you cross a drive and go through another field gate on the opposite side. Walk across a steady slope of meadow towards a large transmitter tower seen on the skyline. On reaching the crown of the slope you will see a small building on the far side. There are distant views of the reservoir as well as others to Goudhurst off to the left.

A few yards to the right of the small building cross a stile in the fence and go straight ahead over the next field to find another stile. Over this turn right and walk along the field edge to a corner with a final stile that brings you to the A21. Again, cross the road with great care to a white lodge building, then wander left along the slip-road back to Pillory Corner Picnic Site.

Items of interest:

1: Bewl Bridge Reservoir. Under the control of Southern Water, the reservoir is the largest inland water south of the Thames. At its northern end there's a large car park and Visitor Centre, and plenty of recreational facilities. Footpaths tour the banks on all sides.

2: Combwell Priory. A handsome stone building, the priory was founded in the late 12th century by Augustinian monks.

The South and East

The south and east of Kent deserve a much larger portion of this book than is given here, but the five routes suggested provide a sample of what is on offer. The countryside is as varied as anywhere in the county, and no less challenging for the walker than areas covered in greater detail. In fact there's much to commend the continuing downs, the towering cliffs of the coastline and lonely wastes of Romney Marsh. Thanet has its appeal, too, an historic region known well to ramblers based in Canterbury and elsewhere in this corner of Kent. Elham's valley is a delight with plenty of footpaths to entice the wanderer (see *Walking in Kent Vol II*). Its stream makes a cheerful companion and there are wild flowers in abundance in the woods and hedgerows. Along breezy clifftops overlooking the sea there are paths leading from one village to another, from town to town and from bay to bay. Each has its own particular character. The Saxon Shore Way explores much that is good on the fringe of the region, and the North Downs Way, of course, has a spur to Canterbury and another to the sea, gaining wonderful airy views from a number of vantage points.

The North Downs are, perhaps, never seen better than along the ridge that hangs over the little agricultural town of Wye. Up there, along the scarp edge, the whole world seems to be spread out below. Inland there are superb scooped valleys with chalk streams bubbling through and woodlands clothing their slopes. It's a quiet, back-of-beyond region, a region with an air of unreality about it that seems somehow divorced from the frenetic world of advanced technology, although no doubt the farmers who tend the land are as hungry as any for the latest development in agricultural science. The wanderer of footpaths, though, sniffs a breeze that contains something of yesterday's world; a world where birdsong and butterflies dominate the day.

Romney Marsh comes as a complete contrast to the soaring downs. A horizontal landscape, it is, bearing a number of isolated churches. For thousands of years the channel tides dashed against cliffs that are now green meadows. One walk is offered that wanders these one-time sea cliffs, and then returns beside the Royal Military Canal on land that once bore ships of peace and of pillage.

*   *   *

WALK 36: WYE - CRUNDALE - COOMBE MANOR - WYE

Distance:	7 miles
Maps:	O.S. Pathfinder 1231 'Ashford & Lyminge' 1:25,000
	O.S. Landranger 179 'Canterbury & East Kent' or 189 'Ashford & Romney Marsh' 1:50,000
Start:	Wye church (GR: 054468)
Access:	About 3 miles north-east of Ashford, off A28. Nearest railway station: Wye
Parking:	Free public car park almost opposite the church
Refreshments:	Pubs and shops in Wye

The Great Stour has forced a passage through the downs between Ashford and Canterbury, and the little township of Wye has grown up on its eastern bank with the North Downs rising as a vast wall behind it. It's splendid walking country; dramatic, peaceful, with huge views from the lip of the downs, or from their folds cupped in a secret heartland of soft valleys where isolated farms and forgotten hamlets lie among the massed orchids of spring, while larks fill the air above with their precious song. This outing explores one such hidden countryside and will make a fine leisurely day's stroll. Don't be tempted to hurry, for this above all will repay a relaxed attitude of mind. There are tremendous views to sit and gaze upon. There will be flowers to study in the shady woods and on the open downs (cowslips, orchids, bluebells, blood-red campion, yellow archangel, the deep blue of bugle, and wild garlic by the acre in spring). And birds to listen to. Butterflies mass the grasslands of summer, silently conducting their business about you, while from the secluded churchyard at Crundale you can wonder that such places still exist - in the 'overcrowded south-east'.

*   *   *

From the main street in Wye (1) enter the churchyard and take the footpath that branches half-right through it, following waymarks

WALK 36

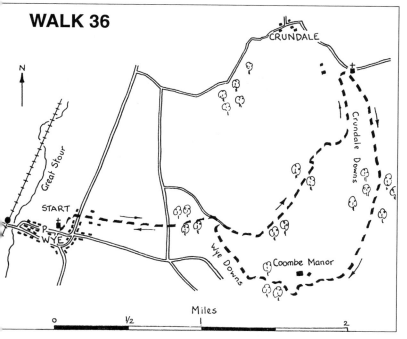

for the North Downs Way and Stour Valley Walk, and at the far side continue between allotments and college buildings. Bear right to cross a narrow road and continue along a driveway aiming for the wall of the downs, passing greenhouses on the left and other buildings of Wye Agricultural College on the right.

The drive becomes a track between fields, and as you progress along it so you may notice a large memorial crown (2) set out in chalk on the downland slope half-right ahead. On the return journey our path will lead above it.

Eventually the track comes to another narrow road, and you continue now on a footpath. At the foot of the downs go through a wooden gate and steeply up a path among trees. At the head of the slope come onto a very narrow lane and turn right. This is glorious folding country now, for on the left of the lane the slope plunges

189

away into a deep green valley that flows off to the north. In the distance can be seen a blocking wall of blue that is another section of the downs. Follow the lane steadily uphill for about 500 yards until you come to a house near the crest of the hill where the lane swings left. Leave it here and continue ahead on a track towards a wood. Enter the woodland through a gate. A footpath then swings left and traces the edge of the woods with Down Farm seen across the neighbouring field. Come out of the woods and wander along the right-hand edge of a field.

Beyond the woods a line of oak trees stretches ahead, leading the path towards a second woodland. Bear slightly left along the edge of this to reach an enclosed corner where a field gate gives access to a path that takes you gently down among trees and flowers and the unseen scrabbling of woodland creatures. Towards the end of the woods it becomes apparent that this pleasant path is leading down a spur of hillside, with valleys stretching ahead on either side.

Out of the trees come to another path that branches off to the right. Do not take this but go ahead on the continuing path that winds leftwards and drops to a junction of tracks (GR: 082476). Turn right here and follow the track to a concrete farm road, then bear left for about 30 yards. Turn right and walk down the edge of a field alongside a row of cypress trees towards the wall of Crundale Downs. At the bottom of the field bear left on a bridleway. In a few paces this eases into the right-hand field and you walk ahead along its bottom edge towards the hamlet of Crundale (3).

The bridleway leads easily along the foot of the downland slope, and with a few houses in view ahead comes to a junction of paths. Cross a stile on the right and climb a steep slope towards Crundale church. At the top of the field bear left for about 30 yards to find another stile across which you come onto a track just below the church (GR: 086486). There are some wonderful views to enjoy here, and the church itself is worth a visit.

Bear right on the track (another bridleway) which takes you along the narrow crest of Crundale Downs, with a lovely valley cutting parallel on either side, and a crown of woods ahead. This is an airy, peaceful walk, serenaded only by the larks overhead or the distant bleating of sheep, and with far-reaching views over a barely inhabited countryside. Come to the edge of a wooded area and continue ahead along its left-hand side. Soon the way leads through Towns Wood, which is magnificent with spring flowers. Eventually the bridleway slopes down to a crossing track. Go straight ahead over a stile almost hidden among trees, and then walk along the right-hand edge of a field. On the far side cross another stile and maintain direction in the next field ahead.

In the far right-hand corner a stile takes the path into and through a woodland corner, then out to a lovely downland slope with the farm buildings of Coombe Manor seen below. Descend towards them, but near the foot of the slope bear left and walk round a fenced boundary to reach a farm access road just to the left of the Manor (GR: 080463). The complex of buildings, set among trees in this peaceful valley, provides an attractive scene.

Turn left along the road and walk towards the head of the valley. After about 120 yards or so you reach the corner of a wood on the right, and leaving the road follow round the edge of the right-hand field with the woodland then on your left, and a fine view down to Coombe Manor below. Come to a field corner where the continuing path cuts up the slope into the woods. At this corner, and leading to it, the ground in spring is covered by great drifts of wild garlic like snowfields of beautiful flowers, their smell heavy and almost overpowering, yet each bloom full of delicate individual stars.

The path emerges from the wood near the head of the slope, and continues across a hilltop field on a walk in the sky. Go through a metal swing gate where the world falls away at your feet. It's a wonderful airy view of plunging downland slope and enormous vistas over a hollow drop, with the flat agricultural land far, far below, and blue hills in the distance. With larks overhead and flowers at your feet, this is indeed a splendid place to sprawl in the grass and dream for an hour. Or so.

To complete the walk bear right along the escarpment with a fence on your right. Soon you come to an undulating stretch with rough pits here and there. Below to the left can be seen the top of the memorial crown. Continue ahead until you reach the edge of a woodland where you turn right, cross a stile and wander along the edge of a field to a narrow lane - recognisable from the outward route. On this bear left and retrace your steps to the wooded path that plunges steeply down the slope to the large open fields beyond which nestles Wye.

Items of interest:

1: Wye. A pleasant little town of timbered cottages, an old watermill on the Great Stour, and a handsome stone-built college given over to the study of agriculture as part of London University. It was built as a college for priests in the 15th century, but became a grammar school in the 18th century, and now trains agricultural students from all over the world. Next to it stands Wye parish church, through whose graveyard goes the North Downs Way.

2: Memorial crown. Seen on the slopes of the downs, this was cut in the chalk by students of Wye College to celebrate the coronation of Edward VII in 1902.

3: Crundale. The remote parish of Crundale covers 1,600 acres, but the 1991 census showed the population as only 175. The church of St Mary, with its flint-studded tower, stands hunched upon its hilltop overlooking the few houses it serves. The present building dates from about the early 13th century, on a site used by the Romans.

WALK 37: WYE DOWNS - HASTINGLEIGH - WYE DOWNS

Distance:	4½ miles
Maps:	O.S. Pathfinder 1231 'Ashford & Lyminge' 1:25,000
	O.S. Landranger 179 'Canterbury & East Kent' or 189 'Ashford & Romney Marsh' 1:50,000
Start:	Wye Downs Nature Reserve (GR: 079453)
Access:	Via Coldharbour Lane; 2 miles out of Wye towards Hastingleigh. The Nature Reserve is an open area on the right
Parking:	Lay-by car park
Refreshments:	Pub in Hastingleigh

Wye Downs National Nature Reserve (1) is a dramatic site with magnificent views overlooking the Weald. The chalk grassland, with its patches of woodland and scrub, provides a rich habitat for wildlife, while numerous wild flower species adorn the meadows right along the scarp edge to attract butterflies that drift through lazy summer days. The site is justifiably popular, and on bright days in spring, summer and autumn the lay-by car park on the Wye-Hastingleigh road is very busy with visitors who potter around the meadows, study the flowers, insects, birds, fly their kites or simply draw breath whilst enjoying the vast panorama spread before them. Our walk, however, deserts the Nature Reserve for the less populous fields, meadows and woodlands away from the scarp edge, but after briefly visiting the secluded village of Hastingleigh, returns to the route of the North Downs Way along the lip of the downs, and finishes with a stroll above the dry valley known as the Devil's Kneading Trough within the Nature Reserve itself.

There is some road walking on this outing, but the country lane is mostly deserted, so there should be little or no traffic to disturb the peace. The majority of the walk explores the less frequented footpaths of this corner of big skies and equally large vistas.

*　*　*

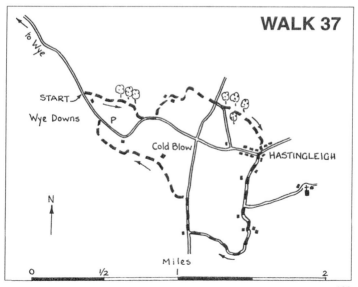

From the lay-by car park walk along the road in the direction of Wye for a short distance, with the fenced area of the Nature Reserve on your left, until you come to the northern entrance to the Devil's Kneading Trough Restaurant (footpath sign). A few paces along the drive cross a stile beside a field gate and walk ahead on the right-hand edge of a field, passing to the left of the restaurant. The way follows a line of pine trees. Just after these finish go through a gap to the right and continue in the same direction along the edge of the adjacent field. The path takes you into Hook's Wood, but soon comes out again and back to the left-hand edge of the field which you follow down to a country road (GR: 084453).

Wander down the road for a short distance, passing the entrance drive to Zig-Zag Farm, seen some way off to the left. Shortly after this cross a stile on the left and walk along the edge of a field to its top left corner where another stile directs the path between a pair of weatherboarded cottages. A grass track leads to a drive where you turn right. About 80 yards later the drive curves to the right. Leave it here and bear left through a gateway into a field, then walk along its right-hand edge for about 150 yards. Turn right through a gateway into the next field where there are two footpaths. Follow the right-hand option straight across the field towards a hedge corner. On reaching this continue in the same direction, soon along the edge of Newlands Wood and onto a country road at a junction (GR: 093455).

Go down the narrow lane opposite, signposted to Hastingleigh and Elmstead. In a few yards the lane forks. Half-left ahead will be seen a footpath cutting into a spinney. Wander through and soon emerge into a field. Walk along the left-hand edge, and when the hedgerow finishes continue in the same direction, now over an open field heading towards a woodland corner. When you reach this continue up the slope with the wood on your left, then through a gateway and onto a grass track where you bear right. This leads alongside some gardens and out at a road in the hamlet of Hastingleigh (2) (GR: 097448).

Turn right and in a few yards come to the village pond and war memorial; an attractive corner. Turn left at the pond and walk down the lane signposted to Hastingleigh church. It's a splendid narrow lane that winds its way at first between a few cottages and past

The heart of Hastingleigh on the North Downs near Wye

Crabtree Farm, with hedgerows bursting with wild flowers in springtime, and folding meadows on either side in the very heart of a downland that holds the secrets of generations of farming families. It's a neat landscape, punctuated with woodlands, fields laid out in a grid of ancient hedges, and with very little habitation to be seen. At the foot of the slope another lane branches left in search of the village church - a long way from the village itself, although footpaths make a short cut to it. We ignore this turning and continue ahead, now climbing the slope beyond. The lane swings left, then right, to pass South Hill Farm, and before long you gain a hint that not far ahead the land will fall steeply away. One senses, rather than sees, that the scarp slope is near.

Shortly after South Hill Farm the lane makes a determined swing to the right, and is joined by the route of the North Downs Way. About a third of a mile later the lane comes to a T junction where you turn right. Some 400 yards or so later reach a stile on the left by a telegraph pole. Over this cross the field to another stile seen

195

on the far side. There are two stiles, in fact. Cross that which is on the right and walk ahead along the left-hand side of a long field, still on the North Downs Way, with the lip of the downs to your left.

A series of stiles and gates leads to the left of Cold Blow Farm. Beyond this continue to follow the North Downs Way. Eventually come to a large wire fence with kennels to the right. The fence-enclosed path goes round to the left, and into a large downland meadow with steep slopes plunging away. You are now in the Wye Downs Nature Reserve. Continue in the same direction, and on reaching a fence cross a stile and bear half-right up the slope, so to come to the road opposite the lay-by car parking area.

Items of interest:

1: Wye Downs Nature Reserve. Stretching for 1^1/$_2$ miles along the scarp face, the National Nature Reserve was established in 1961. It covers 257 hectares and claims a wide variety of plants and wildlife, including 2,000 different insects, 28 different butterflies and some 90 different birds. Of the flowering plants there are 19 species of orchid. The Devil's Kneading Trough is one of several steep-sided coombs moulded by melt-water from the retreating snows of the last Ice Age, around 10,000 years ago. Above it, on the downland meadow, the North Downs Way was officially opened by the Archbishop of Canterbury in a ceremony in 1978.

2: Hastingleigh. A small and largely unspoilt village tucked away on the North Downs to the east of Wye. Its Norman church, somewhat enlarged in the 13th century, stands half a mile away from the village across the fields, or nearly double that by road.

WALK 38: APPLEDORE - KENARDINGTON - WAREHORNE - APPLEDORE

Distance:	7 miles
Maps:	O.S. Pathfinder 1271 'Rye' and 1250 'Tenterden' 1:25,000
	O.S. Landranger 189 'Ashford & Romney Marsh' 1:50,000
Start:	Appledore playing fields, beside B2080 (GR: 955298)

Access:	The playing fields are on the east side of the B2080 (Tenterden-Appledore) road about ¹/₂ mile north of the church. Nearest railway station: Appledore (1¹/₂ miles)
Parking:	With discretion in Appledore High Street
Refreshments:	Pubs in Appledore and Warehorne

This walk explores land that once was sea, and a gentle series of fields and meadows raised a little higher that once overlooked that sea. The area is, of course, on the edge of Romney Marsh, that strange, low-lying region with a character all its own.

At the southernmost corner of the county Romney Marsh contrasts dramatically with almost every other part of Kent. A great flat triangle of meadow and stream, of dyke and ditch, of squat church and wind-bent tree and isolated farms and tiny communities. To south and east its boundaries are the English Channel. Inland, its limit is clearly defined by the long arc of the Royal Military Canal, running from Hythe to Rye, and dug as a defensive measure against possible attack by Napoleon at a time when the Grande Armée was massing at Boulogne. But the threatened invasion never happened, and the canal has never been used for the purpose for which it was created. Some of it now is in the care of the National Trust, with pleasant canal-side paths to enjoy; as on this walk.

First, though, we wander through adjoining fields 'inland' to visit the churches of Kenardington and Warehorne, before joining the route of the Saxon Shore Way for the canal bank walk back to Appledore, with long views across the Marsh country.

*   *   *

Near the northern end of Appledore (1) a footpath signpost directs the start of the walk along the edge of the playing field with houses on the left. On the far side go through a gateway into a field and turn left, then cut diagonally across the field to its far right-hand corner where you will find a stile and a footbridge over a brook. Over this aim half-left across a narrow meadow to another stile seen by a pair of oak trees. Beyond the stile maintain direction up a slope towards a curious mound on the crown of a hill. Pass just to the left of this mound to reach the field boundary. Down the slope slightly left can just be seen Horne's Place (2).

Turn right and walk alongside the boundary fence. Ignore a stile

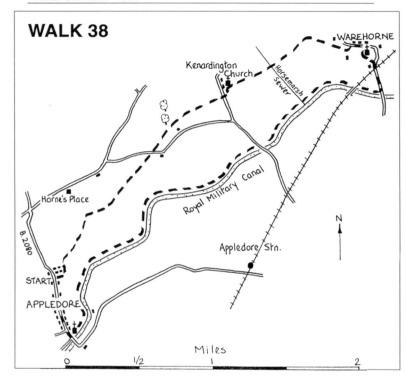

WALK 38

on the left and continue to the end of the hilltop field where a gap in the corner leads into the next large field. The path crosses this slightly left, and in the far corner goes through another gap into a third field. Maintain direction, cross a plank footbridge over a ditch and continue ahead, crossing to a narrow country road (GR: 966314) just to the left of the garden boundary of The Firs.

Cross the road and enter the next field. Maintaining direction come to a band of trees hiding a sunken grass track. A stile takes you into the trees, and two more lead out the other side, with Smith's Farm seen to the right. Go through a small paddock and out to a large open field where you continue in the same direction as before.

This will lead you a little to the right of the brow of the field. In the far distance ahead the tower of Warehorne church can be seen. Using this as a guide continue towards it, and eventually come to a stile in the far boundary, about 30 yards left of a field gate. Over this come onto a narrow country road. Walk into the next field opposite alongside a boundary hedge, then bear left, still alongside the hedge boundary of a garden, and enter the grounds of Kenardington church (3) (GR: 975322) by another stile.

Turn right, walk through the churchyard and out again by yet another stile in the bottom corner. The path leads down to a canal and its accompanying ditches crossed by footbridge. Continue ahead along the left-hand edge of a field, with a line of trees and bushes making a boundary. Shortly before coming to a pond go over a stile on the left, then bear right across a corner to another stile giving access to a field in which a number of rather old apple trees are growing. Cross this half-left to the far corner where a succession of stiles leads into the next field on the right.

Aim towards a point about 50 yards to the right of a house with tall chimneys seen on the far side. Cross a stile in the boundary hedge, walk across the next small field with Warehorne church seen directly ahead, and go through a gate onto a drive. Turn left, then bear right into Warehorne village (4) and enter the churchyard opposite The Woolpack Inn. *(Dodging a downpour we sat in the church porch to eat our sandwiches, and were entertained by a tiny firecrest that perched on a fencepost nearby and preened his feathers undeterred by the heavy rain. If that bright-headed little creature could ignore the weather, then so could we. Inspired, we hunched into our cagoules, and continued with our walk.)*

Do not cross the stile on the right (Saxon Shore Way), but continue round the end of the church. Go through the churchyard and down the slope beyond among old fruit trees, passing to the right of a tennis court and aiming left of a house. There you will find another stile leading directly onto a road. Wander down the road, over a railway level crossing, and soon come to the Royal Military Canal (5).

It is possible to follow the Canal all the way back to Appledore on either bank. The preferred route is along the right bank, mostly following the route of the Saxon Shore Way - which came directly from Warehorne churchyard. This leads along a raised embankment among trees between the Canal on one side and a minor watercourse on the other; a very colourful walk. The left bank option gives broader views over the flat expanse of Romney Marsh, but finishes with a stretch of road walking. The right bank route brings you onto the road just below Appledore church.

Items of interest:

1: Appledore. Once a port, Appledore now stands several miles inland, but it has a flavour of the sea about it. In Saxon times the Danes landed here and 250 longships were drawn up along the Rother's estuary. But King Alfred's diplomacy won the day. In 1380 the French attacked the town and burned the church. The following year Wat Tyler's men marched here with his rebel forces, and Jack Cade did likewise in 1450.

Appledore prospered through the cloth trade, but that prosperity was jeopardised when the River Rother changed course following a violent storm in 1287. That the town survived, and prospered, may be due in some respects to the important market that was held here. On the site of the market place an annual fair was held until 1899. On the approach to the church is a board which gives an interesting potted history of the town.

2: Horne's Place. A farmhouse containing part of a timber-framed house that belonged to William Horne in the 14th century. It was attacked by Wat Tyler in 1381. Next to it stands a very fine domestic chapel built of stone in 1366. Until the 1950s it was used as a barn, but was then restored and is now maintained by English Heritage, and open to the public.

3: Kenardington church. The church of St Mary stands on a knoll overlooking the Marsh country, some way from the village of Kenardington. The tower is Early English in style and dates from 1170. During the 14th century it was burnt by the French, and badly damaged by lightning in 1559, after which both the nave and chancel were taken down. Today the church consists of a west tower and the original south nave aisle; a delightful place.

4: Warehorne A small community standing above the Royal Military Canal, it consists of a handful of houses, a farm or two, The

The Royal Military Canal, Romney Marsh, built as a defence against invasion by Napoleon, but never used as such

Woolpack Inn and a church that has been little altered since the 13th century. The tower, erected in 1776, seems out of place, but within, it is a light, simple place with wooden box pews and pillars of Bethersden marble.

5: Royal Military Canal. In September 1804, William Pitt joined with his military advisers and the Lords and Bailiffs of the Level of Romney Marsh, 'to consider of the best mode of inundating the Marsh in the case of invasion'. Napoleon had gathered his troops at Boulogne, and England was in fear of attack. Martello towers were erected along the coast, and work put in hand to dig a defensive canal, with gun emplacements at strategic points. The Military Canal stretched for 23 miles between Hythe and Rye, and took six years to complete, by which time the invasion scare had long subsided and Pitt was dead.

WALK 39: DENTON - SELSTED - WOOTTON - DENTON

Distance:	5 miles
Maps:	O.S. Pathfinder 1232 'Dover' 1:25,000
	O.S. Landranger 179 'Canterbury & East Kent' 1:50,000
Start:	Denton (GR: 215472)
Access:	Via A260 1½ miles south of A2 near Barham
Parking:	With discretion, in the village
Refreshments:	Pubs in Denton and Wootton

Denton, Selsted and Wootton are all small villages that nestle in a charming 'back of beyond' downland between Canterbury and Dover. Denton and Selsted both stand astride the A260 (which links the Dover road with Folkestone and the Channel Tunnel), but away from the road there are glorious peaceful valleys with hardly any habitation; a land of big fields and meadows where larks rise with joyful song, and wood-crowned hills are loud with jackdaws. A number of footpaths score across this folding countryside, to entice the walker into a discovery of this secret Kent. The circular walk offered here is just one of several possibilities. Once you've had a glimpse of what's on offer, study the map for further explorations.

*   *   *

From The Jackdaw pub in the main street of Denton cross the road and veer slightly left along a narrow lane/driveway between houses, to reach the Village Hall. Pass to the left of this and enter a sloping field. Walk up the field along its right-hand boundary, and enter a corner of Willow Wood by a telegraph pole. The path winds through before emerging into an open field on the right. Bear left and walk alongside the continuing wood, then over a stile into a hilltop field whose left-hand boundary is lined with a woodland shaw. Cross two hilltop fields walking parallel with the shaw. The buildings of Snodehill Farm are seen ahead and to the right. On the far side of the second field come to a narrow country lane and bear left (GR: 206465).

WALK 39

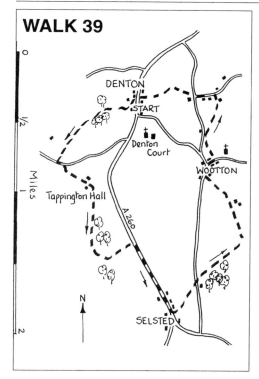

A few paces later go through a gap into a sloping field on the right. Wander down the slope, half-left, pass through a gap among trees at the bottom of the field, and come to a crossing track. Walk ahead down a farm drive leading to an attractive old farmhouse, Tappington Hall (1). Go through the farmyard, and when the drive curves sharply left, ignore the stile ahead and veer half-right on a track. Through a gateway walk up the slope aiming for the right-hand side of a woodland crown, with lovely views into the valley on the right, and with a charming countryside of folding hills all around.

With Summer House Wood on your left walk along the hilltop, and a few paces beyond overhead power cables, bear left through a narrowing of the wood. Out the other side maintain direction down into a narrow, shallow valley, then up the opposite slope in a clearing through Denton Wood. At the head of the slope, just beyond a pylon, come onto the A260. Turn right and walk along the road with care (there's no footway for quite a distance) for a little over ¹/₂ mile towards the village of Selsted.

Pass a couple of handsome thatched cottages and a few more houses, then as the road makes a right-hand bend turn left among trees to a stile giving access to a small field. Wander across to a second stile, over which you follow the left-hand hedgerow edging a larger field. When the hedge finishes continue ahead, making for the bottom left-hand corner of the field where, after going through some more trees, you come to another very narrow country road (GR: 222452).

Cross the road to find a continuing footpath by a very small pond. The path climbs a tree-tangled slope, but soon improves alongside Park Wood. At the end of the first field cross a stile into the next, a long open field that stretches beyond Park Wood with a fence as its right-hand boundary. Two-thirds of the way along this come to a crossing path (not always evident on the ground - depending on the crop being grown) and bear half-left towards the left-hand end of three large grey barns. Having reached them go through a gate onto a concrete farm road. Directly ahead find a stile in the hedge, and over this walk down a short field to a second stile found to the left of a group of trees.

Aim half-right up the next field, over another stile where you bear left aiming for houses seen at the far side of the field. Two more stiles take you to an enclosed footpath leading directly onto a road in Wootton (2). Turn right into the village, soon passing The Endeavour pub on your right. Just beyond this bear left (signpost) on a track down the side of a bungalow, and enter a field.

Walk along the right-hand edge to the bottom corner. Veer slightly right among trees, then over a stile walk down the next field (a gentle rolling countryside) with Shelvin Farm seen in the distance. Halfway down the slope go through a field gate and pass to the left of a barn to reach a narrow country lane by Park Farm. Bear left and walk up the lane until you reach a T junction (GR: 222473).

Turn right for a few paces, then through a gap on the left and up a slope into the corner of a field (a house to your left). Cross the field diagonally to its top right-hand corner, and you'll find a stile just to the right of a group of trees. Over this bear left and in a few paces cross another stile leading into a shaw of bushes and trees. Emerge from these into a sloping field overlooking the village of Denton in its neat valley. Wander straight down through the field to the car park of The Jackdaw pub.

Items of interest:

1: Tappington Hall. This fine Jacobean farmhouse was built about 1628 and featured in one of Richard Barham's *Ingoldsby Legends*. In *The Spectre of Tappington* Barham described it as "an antiquated but commodious manor house." Barham himself actually inherited Tappington Hall at the age of seven.

2: Wootton. The earliest reference to the village appears in a document of A.D. 687 where the name is spelt Uudetun. The flint-walled church of St Martin dates largely from the early 13th century, and has a lovely ancient yew tree at its entrance.

WALK 40: DOVER (LANGDON CLIFFS) - ST MARGARET'S AT CLIFFE - LANGDON CLIFFS

Distance:	6¹/₂ miles
Maps:	O.S. Pathfinder 1232 'Dover' 1:25,000
	O.S. Landranger 179 'Canterbury & East Kent' 1:50,000
Start:	Langdon Cliffs Picnic Site (GR: 335422)
Access:	Via signposted minor road branching east of A258 1 mile south of A2 roundabout (Jubilee Way)
Parking:	Langdon Cliffs Picnic Site
Refreshments:	Pubs and café in St Margaret's at Cliffe, kiosk at Langdon Cliffs

The white cliffs of Dover have represented the gateway to England for centuries. They've been celebrated in literature, in song, on countless photographs and paintings. Seen from a home-bound Channel ferry they symbolise more than just an upthrusting wall of chalk; to the invading Romans they must have seemed impregnable. Above Dover the massive castle that overlooks the town and the Channel itself was England's second line of defence after the cliffs themselves. Not even Hitler's bombardment during the last war could raze it to the ground, and it remains today as defiant as the cliffs on which it stands. This walk captures an airy glimpse of the white cliffs as we wander along their green turf brow - and with Dover Castle in view now and then.

However, the clifftop walk represents only the second half of this outing, for the first part explores a slightly tilted land of big fields with big skies stretched over all. It's a very pleasant cross-country section and a leisurely introduction to the more dramatic return walk from St Margaret's. Coming back along the clifftop path the French coast is easily discerned on a clear day. There's much coming and going of Channel ferries and hovercraft, but even without that seabound traffic there will be plenty to attract interest: lighthouses, a windmill, a coastguard's station, the flower-starred turf, birdsong, rabbit activity - and the dazzle of sun on water.

*   *   *

Leave the picnic site car park by walking back towards Dover on the minor road by which you cross the deep cut of the A2, with very fine views of Dover Castle (1) ahead. Immediately after having crossed the roadbridge, go down a slope on the right and over a stile into the bottom edge of a sloping field. Walk ahead, parallel with the A2, following the right-hand fence. Towards the end of the field veer slightly left to a gate in the field corner. Through this bear left along a track, walking towards a bungalow and two barns. Pass between the barns and up to the A258 road where you turn right to gain a roundabout on the A2 (Jubilee Way).

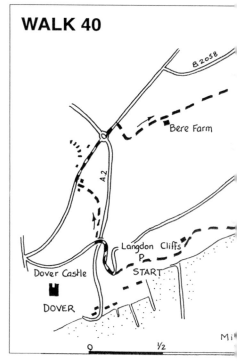

WALK 40

B 2058

Bere Farm

A2

Langdon Cliffs
P.
Dover Castle
START

DOVER

0   ½   Mi

206

Cross straight ahead with care, and maintain direction along the continuing A258 for about 150 yards. Now cross a stile into a field on the right and walk along its left headland. In another 150 yards cross a stile on the left. There are two brick pillboxes nearby. Walk straight ahead along the right-hand edge of a field, and on reaching its far corner come to a track by Bere Farm (GR: 337437). Over the track maintain direction alongside a flint-walled barn. Pass more farm buildings, go through a gate and veer slightly left into a field.

The way leads to the far right-hand corner, at first crossing the near-corner, then along the right headland. Reaching the far corner

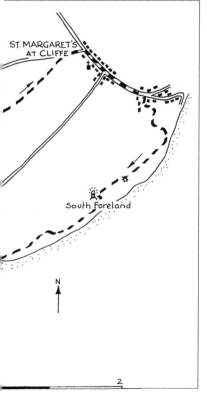

cross another stile and head slightly right across an open field. On the far side go over another stile and continue in the same direction to yet another stile. Having crossed this you then follow the left-hand fenceline. Eventually this brings you to a track (more pillboxes) on the line of a disused railway built during the last war. The track leads directly to a road, and you walk ahead to reach a T junction (Station Road). Bear right into the centre of St Margaret's at Cliffe (2).

Walking through St Margaret's, Station Road becomes Sea Street, the road which leads to St Margaret's Bay (3). This is the B2058. A little under ¹/₂ mile beyond the church the road forks by a green. Ahead the road begins its descent to St Margaret's Bay, but we turn right into St Margaret's Road. About 50 yards later turn left down a concrete drive. When this curves left to

The White House, go straight ahead down a flight of steps enclosed between a wall and a fence, and at the bottom turn right into Foreland Road. In 100 yards fork left on a track. Come to cross-tracks and continue ahead, ignoring a footpath half-right. The track now rises among trees and bushes, then curves right onto Lighthouse Down near the cliff edge.

Now following the Saxon Shore Way remain on the track heading south-west for about ³/₄ mile, passing to the right of St Margaret's Windmill (4) surrounded by trees, and a disused lighthouse. Just before coming to a narrow road, leave the track for a footpath on the left among bushes, then alongside a hedge towards a large lighthouse (South Foreland). Turn left on a narrow footpath by the lighthouse entrance gates and wander down towards the cliff edge.

The clifftop path now veers right. Far off you can see Dungeness Nuclear Power Station standing on its gravel projection; nearer to hand are the lovely plunging white cliffs, and as you progress along the path, so Dover Harbour comes into view. The French coast makes an undulating line across the Channel on a clear day, and there's a constant traffic of ferry boats and hovercraft plying this busiest of all the world's waterways.

The path curves round a neat green amphitheatre, or dry valley (Fan Point), and soon after there are alternative trails being offered. Remain on the lower (cliff-side) path with a large coastguard building seen ahead. Waymarks lead towards it, over a broad track (this also once carried a railway line) and up a flight of wood-braced steps. Keeping just to the left of the building, follow a fence on your left, go through a gate and wander across Langdon Cliffs with their fine views onto Dover Harbour below, and so reach the picnic site and car park.

Items of interest:

1: Dover Castle. Built by the Normans 465 feet above the sea, the walls are 21 feet thick at their base and the keep is 91 feet high. At the time it was built it cost the astonishing sum of £7,000, and until recently it had been continuously garrisoned for 800 years. In a field below the castle a granite outline of a plane marks the spot where Frenchman Louis Bleriot landed his monoplane in July 1909, after making the first powered flight across the English Channel.

2: St Margaret's at Cliffe. The church of St Margaret of Antioch has one of the largest Norman towers in the county, and some fine carvings round the west door. One of the stained glass windows is a memorial to those who perished in the *Herald of Free Enterprise* disaster, when that ferry capsized off Zeebrugge in 1988. Three of the crew members who died were from St Margarets.

3: St Margaret's Bay. Traditionally St Margaret's Bay has been the starting (or finishing) point for cross-Channel swimmers. During World War II the famous naval guns, nicknamed Winnie and Pooh, fired salvos from here across the Channel to France. Since 1972 a statue of Sir Winston Churchill has overlooked the bay, peering defiantly across the water.

4: St Margaret's Windmill. This handsome smock mill was built in 1928, but it was only in use for 11 years, and ceased operations in 1939.

Long-distance Paths

A number of long-distance walking routes pass through Kent, thereby enabling keen ramblers opportunities to discover parts of the county that remain forever the preserve of those prepared to forsake the tarmac highways. Some of these routes have been developed or promoted by bodies like the Countryside Commission and the Ramblers' Association, others have been actively pursued by Kent County Council. All are worth considering.

Most have been created by linking existing rights of way wherever possible, together with the odd short stretch of green lane or country road where no paths exist. Some LDPs may have no more than conventional finger posts or slim direction arrows as their waymark, but the majority have their own identifying symbol; a blue overlapping WW signifies the Wealdway, for example, a red Viking helmet the Saxon Shore Way, an acorn symbol for the North Downs Way.

Tackling a multi-day route is a fine experience, and there can be few better ways of getting to the very heart of the countryside than this. Day after day the journey leads through an ever-changing landscape, giving a variety of scenery and an increasingly broad perspective. Some routes follow a particular geological feature, such as the North Downs Way, while others (the Wealdway is a good example) cross one range of hills after another, from one valley system to the next, with all the differences in vegetation cover that this entails. The long-distance walker thereby gains much from the experience besides the obvious sense of achievement that comes with the route's completion.

The following list of LDPs in Kent gives only the briefest of details, but anyone wishing to find out more about a specific route is advised to consult the guidebook recommended for that particular walk.

*   *   *

1: THE GREENSAND WAY

Distance:	110 miles
Start:	Haslemere (Surrey) *Finish:* Hamstreet (nr Ashford)
Guidebooks:	A series of route cards are available for the Surrey section; apply in local bookshops or libraries. For the Kent section *Greensand Way in Kent* by Bea Cowan (pb KCC)

As its name implies, the GW follows the ridge of the Lower Greensand across Surrey and Kent, through some of the most spectacular countryside in the south. It enters Kent on Crockham Hill and heads eastward along the ridge to Toys Hill, Ide Hill and Knole Park at Sevenoaks. On the way to Ightham Mote it deserts the ridge itself, but traverses the southern slopes with continuing interest and delightful vistas. Having crossed the Medway at Yalding the route regains the crest deep in orchard country, explores tiny hamlets and neat parklands on its curve towards the south, and at Hamstreet joins the Saxon Shore Way. Several walks described in this book follow sections of the GW.

2: THE LONDON COUNTRYWAY

Distance:	205 miles
Start/Finish:	Box Hill (Surrey)
Guidebook:	*A London Countryway* by Keith Chesterton (pb Constable)

The walker's M25, this is a circular route that explores the immediate countryside around London, varying from 13 to 31 miles from the city centre. Entering Kent from Essex via the Tilbury-Gravesend ferry, it then heads south into the chalklands of the North Downs, drops over the scarp edge, veers clockwise towards the west, and up onto the Greensand Ridge. The London Countryway crosses the route of several other LDPs in Kent, and is met on one or two of the walks mentioned in this guide.

3: THE NORTH DOWNS WAY

Distance:	153 miles
Start:	Farnham (Surrey) *Finish:* Dover (or Canterbury)
Guidebooks:	*A Guide to the Pilgrims Way & North Downs Way* by Christopher John Wright (pb Constable) is perhaps the best of several guides to this route. Also useful is: *The North Downs Way - A User's Guide* (pb KCC)

A splendid route, spoilt in places only by the close proximity of busy motorways, it enjoys some spectacular sections and surprisingly remote parts of the countryside. From Surrey the NDW comes into Kent above Westerham, crosses the Darent Gap to Otford and climbs again onto the lip of the downs high above Kemsing. At Rochester it crosses the Medway on an airy bridge, and arcs towards the south-east. Later the Way forks; one route heads through Wye and on over the downs in one of the finest sections of all, to Folkestone and Dover; the alternative spur goes into orchard country and finishes at Canterbury. Again, several walks described in this book follow parts of the North Downs Way.

4: THE PILGRIMS' WAY

Distance:	118 miles
Start:	Winchester (Hants) *Finish:* Canterbury
Guidebook:	*A Guide to the Pilgrims Way & North Downs Way* by Christopher John Wright (pb Constable)

The traditional route taken by Christian pilgrims linking what was the secular capital of England with the ecclesiastical centre, there are doubts as to the authenticity of its origins. Not that this matters one jot to the walker! The route has existed for centuries, but has largely been superceded as a modern long-distance walking route by the North Downs Way with which it shares a number of footpaths and trackways. Some of the modern Pilgrims' Way is along country roads and green lanes.

5: THE SAXON SHORE WAY

Distance:	135 miles
Start:	Gravesend *Finish:* Rye (Sussex)
Guidebooks:	*The Saxon Shore Way* by Alan Sillitoe and Fay Godwin (pb Hutchinson); *The Saxon Shore Way* (published in 10 sections) available from local bookshops, tourist information centres, or from: Mr P. Miller, Kent Area RA, 104 Hamelin Road, Darland, Gillingham, Kent ME7 3ER

This LDP runs for almost its entire length within the county's boundaries, straying only into East Sussex at the very end. It is both a long-distance walking route and a history trail, for it follows as far as is possible the coastline as it was in Saxon times, and on the way passes a number of sites of historic interest. The shoreline is also of considerable interest to naturalists, especially along the Swale where birdlife is plentiful.

6: A SOUTH COAST WAY

Distance:	81 miles
Start:	Dover *Finish:* Eastbourne (Sussex)
Guidebook:	*A South Coast Way* by Laurence Main (pb Thornhill Press)

Linking the North Downs Way with the South Downs Way, this route traces the shoreline wherever possible - sometimes a few miles inland - and visits Folkestone, Hythe, New Romney, and over the border in Sussex to Rye, Hastings and Pevensey before reaching Eastbourne. There are clifftop sections, sea walls and canal banks, and some historic sites along the way.

7: SUSSEX BORDER PATH

Distance:	150 miles
Start:	Emsworth (Sussex) *Finish:* Rye (Sussex)
Guidebook:	*The Sussex Border Path* by Ben Perkins and Aeneas Mackintosh (route folder with 9 separate sheets) available from: Ben Perkins, 11 Old London Road, Brighton BN1 8XR

Wherever possible this route tours the county boundaries of East and West Sussex, but by its very nature it strays into neighbouring counties. As far as Kent is concerned, it enters near Cowden and Ashurst, and east of Bewl Bridge Reservoir near Hawkhurst as well as other areas too. Some of the walks in this book share parts of this LDP.

8: THE VANGUARD WAY

Distance:	62 miles
Start:	East Croydon (Surrey) *Finish:* Seaford Head (Sussex)
Guidebooks:	*The Vanguard Way* (pb The Vanguards Rambling Club); *The Wealdway & The Vanguard Way* by Kev Reynolds (pb Cicerone Press)

Developed by Croydon-based Vanguards Rambling Club in 1980, this sets out to walk from the suburbs of London to the clifftop of Seaford Head overlooking the Channel. On the way it crosses the North Downs, Greensand Ridge, goes through the Weald and over Ashdown Forest before coming to the South Downs and the coast. A fine walk along footpaths and quiet country lanes, it enters Kent near Crockham Hill and walks south near the Surrey border before leaving the county near the glorious viewpoint of Dry Hill.

9: THE WEALDWAY

Distance:	82 miles
Start:	Gravesend *Finish:* Beachy Head (Sussex)
Guidebook:	*The Wealdway & The Vanguard Way* by Kev Reynolds (pb Cicerone Press)

From the River Thames to the English Channel, the Wealdway is a truly fine walk that crosses some of the best and most deserted countryside in the south. On leaving Gravesend it soon enters the back-country of the North Downs, then drops over the scarp slope towards the Greensand Ridge. From there into the Weald and along the Medway to Tonbridge, onto a High Weald ridge at Bidborough and through rolling countryside to Southborough and Fordcombe. Near Ashurst the LDP enters Sussex to cross Ashdown Forest and continues to the South Downs and the sea.

* * *

KKC Sponsored Routes

In recent years Kent County Council has pursued a policy of encouraging greater use of the footpath network that exists in the county, through the development of a number of walking routes, and upgrading of certain permissive paths to public rights of way. The following list details linear routes sponsored by the Council. All guides mentioned are published by KCC.

1: Darent Valley Path
A 15-mile walk linking Dartford with Sevenoaks (Riverhead or Chipstead) along the banks of the River Darent wherever possible. A number of places of interest along the way, including Lullingstone Roman Villa.
Countryside Walks in North West Kent is a pack of four linking circular walks and a leaflet covering the DVP.

2: Eden Valley Walk
From Edenbridge to Tonbridge, linking the Vanguard Way and Wealdway (see above), the Eden Valley walk is 15 miles long. Along the valleys of the Eden and Medway it visits Hever and Penshurst, and enjoys some fine landscapes.
Eden Valley Walk by Caroline Wing describes places of interest along the way.

3: Elham Valley Way
The splendid Elham Valley cuts through the North Downs between Canterbury and Hythe (see recommended routes described in *Walking in Kent Vol II*). This recreational route of 23 miles explores some of the finest countryside of East Kent.
Elham Valley Way was published in 1994.

4: High Weald Walk
A 27$^{1}/_{2}$ mile circular route passing through the High Weald Area of Outstanding Natural Beauty - a ring round Tunbridge Wells, straying into East Sussex too. *High Weald Walk* by Bea Cowan was published in 1994.

5: Medway River Path

This walk is almost entirely along the Medway towpath, linking Tonbridge with Rochester. The route strays from the river bank downstream from Aylesford, but rejoins the right bank for a final stroll into Rochester. The walk is about 27 miles long, and there's plenty of interest all the way. (Walk 28 in this guidebook describes the route from Tonbridge to Maidstone.) At the time of writing KCC are finalising rights of way before publishing their guidebook: *Medway River Path* by Kev Reynolds.

6: Stour Valley Walk

Following the Great Stour River for 35 miles between Ashford and Sandwich, in places the route makes a diversion from the river itself, but always for good reasons. The walk visits Wye, Canterbury, Fordwich and Richborough; fine scenery and plenty of historic interest.

Stour Valley Walk is written by G. Allanson, C. Donaldson, R. Lloyd and K. Snelson.

All the above guides should be available from local bookshops, tourist information offices, or by post from: Access & Recreation Officer, KCC Planning Department, Springfield, Maidstone ME14 2LX.

*   *   *

APPENDIX A

Useful Addresses:

1: Kent County Council (Planning Dept)
   Springfield
   Maidstone
   ME14 2LX

2: Kent Trust for Nature Conservation
   Tyland Barn
   PO Box 29
   Maidstone

3: The National Trust
   (Kent & East Sussex Regional Office)
   Scotney Castle, Lamberhurst
   Tunbridge Wells

4: Ramblers' Association
   1-5 Wandsworth Road
   London
   SW8 2LJ

5: English Heritage
   PO Box 1BB
   London
   W1A 1BB

6: South-East England Tourist Board
   1 Warwick Park
   Tunbridge Wells
   TN2 5TA

7: YHA (England & Wales)
   Trevelyan House
   8 St Stephen's Hill
   St Albans, Herts
   AL1 2DY

APPENDIX B

Recommended Further Reading:

Belloc, H.	*The Old Road* (Constable)
Bignell, A.	*The Kent Village Book* (Countryside Books)
	Kent Lore (Robert Hale)
Church, R.	*Kent* (Robert Hale)
Cobbett, W.	*Rural Rides*
Glover, J.	*The Place Names of Kent* (Batsford)
Kaye-Smith, S.	*Weald of Kent & Sussex* (Robert Hale)
Margary, I.D.	*Roman Ways in the Weald* (Dent)
Mason, O.	*South-East England* (Bartholomew)
Maxwell, D.	*Unknown Kent* (Bodley Head)
Mee, A.	*The King's England - Kent* (Hodder & Stoughton)
Newman, J.	*North-East and East Kent* The Buildings of England series, Pevsner, N. (ed) (Penguin)
Nicolson, N.	*Kent* (Wiedenfeld & Nicolson)
Reynolds, K.	*The Visitor's Guide to Kent* (Moorland Publishing)
	Walking in Kent Vol II (Cicerone Press)
	Classic Walks in Southern England (Oxford Illustrated Press)
Spence, K.	*The Companion Guide to Kent & Sussex* (Collins)
Vigar, J.	*Exploring Kent Churches* (Meresborough Books)
Webb, W.	*Kent's Historic Buildings* (Robert Hale)

CICERONE GUIDES
Cicerone publish a wide range of reliable guides to walking and climbing in Britain, and other general interest books.

LAKE DISTRICT - General Books
CONISTON COPPER A History
CHRONICLES OF MILNTHORPE
A DREAM OF EDEN -LAKELAND DALES
EDEN TAPESTRY
THE HIGH FELLS OF LAKELAND
LAKELAND - A taste to remember (Recipes)
LAKELAND VILLAGES
LAKELAND TOWNS
THE LAKERS
THE LOST RESORT? (Morecambe)
LOST LANCASHIRE (Furness area)
OUR CUMBRIA Stories of Cumbrian Men and Women
THE PRIORY OF CARTMEL
REFLECTIONS ON THE LAKES
AN ILLUSTRATED COMPANION INTO LAKELAND

LAKE DISTRICT - Guide Books
THE BORDERS OF LAKELAND
BIRDS OF MORECAMBE BAY
CASTLES IN CUMBRIA
CONISTON COPPER MINES Field Guide
THE CUMBRIA CYCLE WAY
THE EDEN WAY
IN SEARCH OF WESTMORLAND
SHORT WALKS IN LAKELND-1: SOUTH LAKELAND
SCRAMBLES IN THE LAKE DISTRICT
MORE SCRAMBLES IN THE LAKE DISTRICT
THE TARNS OF LAKELAND VOL 1 - WEST
WALKING ROUND THE LAKES
WALKS IN SILVERDALE/ARNSIDE
WESTMORLAND HERITAGE WALK
WINTER CLIMBS IN THE LAKE DISTRICT

NORTHERN ENGLAND (outside the Lakes
BIRDWATCHING ON MERSEYSIDE
CANAL WALKS Vol 1 North
CANOEISTS GUIDE TO THE NORTH EAST
THE CLEVELAND WAY & MISSING LINK
THE DALES WAY
DOUGLAS VALLEY WAY
WALKING IN THE FOREST OF BOWLAND
HADRIANS VOL 1 The Wall Walk
HERITAGE TRAILS IN NW ENGLAND
THE ISLE OF MAN COASTAL PATH
IVORY TOWERS & DRESSED STONES (Follies)
THE LANCASTER CANAL
LANCASTER CANAL WALKS
A WALKERS GUIDE TO THE LANCASTER CANAL
LAUGHS ALONG THE PENNINE WAY
A NORTHERN COAST-TO-COAST
NORTH YORK MOORS Walks
THE REIVERS WAY (Northumberland)
THE RIBBLE WAY
ROCK CLIMBS LANCASHIRE & NW
WALKING DOWN THE LUNE
WALKING IN THE SOUTH PENNINES
WALKING IN THE NORTH PENNINES
WALKING IN THE WOLDS
WALKS IN THE YORKSHIRE DALES (3 VOL)
WALKS IN LANCASHIRE WITCH COUNTRY
WALKS IN THE NORTH YORK MOORS (2 VOL)
WALKS TO YORKSHIRE WATERFALLS (2 vol)
WATERFALL WALKS -TEESDALE & THE HIGH PENNINES
WALKS ON THE WEST PENNINE MOORS
WALKING NORTHERN RAILWAYS (2 vol)
THE YORKSHIRE DALES A walker's guide

Also a full range of EUROPEAN and OVERSEAS guidabooks - walking, long distance trails, scrambling, ice-climbing, rock climbing.

DERBYSHIRE & EAST MIDLANDS
KINDER LOG
HIGH PEAK WALKS
WHITE PEAK WAY
WHITE PEAK WALKS - 2 Vols
WEEKEND WALKS IN THE PEAK DISTRICT
THE VIKING WAY
THE DEVIL'S MILL / WHISTLING CLOUGH (Novels)

WALES & WEST MIDLANDS
ASCENT OF SNOWDON
WALKING IN CHESHIRE
CLWYD ROCK
HEREFORD & THE WYE VALLEY A Walker's Guide
HILLWALKING IN SNOWDONIA
HILL WALKING IN WALES (2 Vols)
THE MOUNTAINS OF ENGLAND & WALES Vol 1 WALES
WALKING OFFA'S DYKE PATH
THE RIDGES OF SNOWDONIA
ROCK CLIMBS IN WEST MIDLANDS
SARN HELEN Walking Roman Road
SCRAMBLES IN SNOWDONIA
SEVERN WALKS
THE SHROPSHIRE HILLS A Walker's Guide
SNOWDONIA WHITE WATER SEA & SURF
WALKING DOWN THE WYE
WELSH WINTER CLIMBS

SOUTH & SOUTH WEST ENGLAND
WALKING IN THE CHILTERNS
COTSWOLD WAY
COTSWOLD WALKS (3 VOLS)
WALKING ON DARTMOOR
WALKERS GUIDE TO DARTMOOR PUBS
EXMOOR & THE QUANTOCKS
THE KENNET & AVON WALK
LONDON THEME WALKS
AN OXBRIDGE WALK
A SOUTHERN COUNTIES BIKE GUIDE
THE SOUTHERN-COAST-TO-COAST
SOUTH DOWNS WAY & DOWNS LINK
SOUTH WEST WAY - 2 Vol
THE TWO MOORS WAY Dartmoor-Exmoor
WALKS IN KENT Bk 2
THE WEALDWAY & VANGUARD WAY

SCOTLAND
THE BORDER COUNTRY - WALKERS GUIDE
BORDER PUBS & INNS A Walker's Guide
CAIRNGORMS WINTER CLIMBS
WALKING THE GALLOWAY HILLS
THE ISLAND OF RHUM
THE SCOTTISH GLENS (Mountainbike Guide)
    Book 1:THE CAIRNGORM GLENS
    Book 2 THE ATHOLL GLENS
    Book 3 THE GLENS OF RANNOCH
SCOTTISH RAILWAY WALKS
SCRAMBLES IN LOCHABER
SCRAMBLES IN SKYE
SKI TOURING IN SCOTLAND
TORRIDON A Walker's Guide
WALKS from the WEST HIGHLAND RAILWAY
WINTER CLIMBS BEN NEVIS & GLENCOE

REGIONAL BOOKS UK & IRELAND
THE ALTERNATIVE PENNINE WAY
CANAL WALKS Vol.1: North
LIMESTONE - 100 BEST CLIMBS
THE PACKHORSE BRIDGES OF ENGLAND
THE RELATIVE HILLS OF BRITAIN
THE MOUNTAINS OF ENGLAND & WALES
    VOL 1 WALES, VOL 2 ENGLAND
THE MOUNTAINS OF IRELAND

Other guides are constantly being added to the Cicerone List.
Available from bookshops, outdoor equipment shops or direct (send s.a.e. for price list) from
CICERONE, 2 POLICE SQUARE, MILNTHORPE, CUMBRIA, LA7 7PY